Mystic Ruminations

Azariah Samuel A

Published by Azariah Samuel A, 2024.

While every precaution has been taken in the preparation of this book, the publisher assumes no responsibility for errors or omissions, or for damages resulting from the use of the information contained herein.

MYSTIC RUMINATIONS

First edition. October 3, 2024.

ISBN: 979-8227401434

Written by Azariah Samuel A.

Table of Contents

MYSTIC RUMINATIONS

Divine Flirtations and Enchanted Conversations with The Eternal

A Journey Through the Wisdom of Rumi

Azariah Samuel A

PRAISE FOR THE MYSTIC RUMINATIONS

1.   Elena Michaels, author of "Whispers of the Soul":

"A mesmerizing journey into the heart of Rumi's wisdom. 'Mystic Ruminations' captures the essence of divine love and spiritual longing with unparalleled beauty and grace."

1.   David Lawson, New York Times Bestselling Author of "Echoes of Eternity":

"Azariah's eloquent prose weaves a tapestry of spiritual insights that illuminate the timeless teachings of Rumi. This book is a treasure for anyone seeking to deepen their connection with the divine."

1.   Sophia Bennett, author of "Celestial Harmonies":

"Reading 'Mystic Ruminations' feels like a dance with the divine. Azariah's reflections on Rumi's teachings are both profound and deeply moving."

1.   Jonathan Clarke, author of "Pathways to the Infinite":

"Azariah brings Rumi's mystical wisdom to life with poetic brilliance and heartfelt reverence. This book is a beacon of light for spiritual seekers."

1.   Isabella Grant, author of "The Eternal Embrace":

"'Mystic Ruminations' is a soul-stirring exploration of love and spirituality. Azariah's interpretations of Rumi's words are both insightful and transformative."

1.   Marcus Dean, author of "Beyond the Veil":

"A masterful blend of poetic elegance and spiritual depth. Azariah's 'Mystic Ruminations' offers a profound journey into the heart of Rumi's teachings."

1. Lila Hayes, author of "Sacred Whispers":

"Azariah's exquisite prose and deep understanding of Rumi's wisdom make 'Mystic Ruminations' an essential read for anyone on a spiritual path."

1. Alexander Carter, author of "Infinite Horizons":

"'Mystic Ruminations' is a beautiful and inspiring tribute to Rumi's legacy. Azariah's insights are both enlightening and deeply touching."

1. Nina Rodriguez, author of "Divine Echoes":

"Azariah captures the essence of Rumi's teachings with profound clarity and poetic grace. 'Mystic Ruminations' is a must-read for lovers of spiritual literature."

1. Ethan Powell, author of "Awakening the Soul":

"A breathtaking exploration of the divine through the eyes of Rumi. Azariah's 'Mystic Ruminations' is a luminous guide to spiritual awakening."

1. Olivia Martin, author of "Soulful Reflections":

"'Mystic Ruminations' is a beautifully crafted journey into the heart of Rumi's wisdom. Azariah's words resonate with the timeless truths of the soul."

1. Henry Blake, author of "Eternal Light":

"Azariah's profound understanding of Rumi's teachings shines through every page of 'Mystic Ruminations.' This book is a testament to the transformative power of divine love."

1. Amelia Scott, author of "Celestial Visions":

"'Mystic Ruminations' is a poetic and spiritual masterpiece. Azariah's reflections on Rumi's wisdom are both captivating and enlightening."

1.   Lucas Reed, author of "Sacred Pathways":

"Azariah's 'Mystic Ruminations' is a profound and inspiring exploration of Rumi's teachings. This book is a beacon of light for all spiritual seekers."

1.   Grace Thompson, author of "Eternal Journey":

"'Mystic Ruminations' is a soul-stirring tribute to Rumi's legacy. Azariah's insights are both profound and deeply moving, offering a transformative journey into the heart of the divine."

MYSTIC RUMINATIONS

Divine Flirtations and Enchanted Conversations with The Eternal

A Journey Through the Wisdom of Rumi

Azariah Samuel A

God is Love, God is Gracious, God is Merciful, God is Infinitely Incomprehensible, God is Almighty.

Acknowledgements

This book is dedicated to my father, whose unwavering support and boundless wisdom have been my guiding light. Dad, your profound understanding of life and your endless encouragement have inspired every word within these pages. Your love and belief in me have been the foundation upon which this work stands.

I also extend my deepest gratitude to my beloved wife, whose patience, love, and unwavering faith in me have been a source of constant strength. Your gentle guidance and enduring support have allowed me to pursue my passion with unwavering determination.

To my incredible work partners, Samuel Raj and Salma, your dedication, creativity, and tireless efforts have been instrumental in bringing this book to life. Your insights and hard work have enriched this project in countless ways.

A heartfelt thanks to all my colleagues and friends who have contributed to this journey. Your encouragement and collaboration have made this endeavor a truly enriching experience.

To all of you, I am deeply grateful for your belief in me and for your contributions, both big and small. This book is as much yours as it is mine. Thank you for being a part of this incredible journey. Thank you all for being a part of this incredible journey.

With gratitude,
Azariah Samuel A

In verses spun with mystic grace,
Rumi's words, a sacred space.
Each line a dance with love divine,
A whisper from the heart's true shrine.
His pen ignites a soulful fire,
With passion's flame, it lifts us higher.
Enchanted talks with the Eternal,
Reveal the beauty of the internal.
Divine love flows in every word,
A symphony of hearts that's heard.
Mystical delight in every rhyme,
Eternity touched, transcending time.
Through Rumi's eyes, the world anew,
In love's embrace, all souls he drew.
A literary power so profound,
In his wisdom, peace is found.

- Azariah Samuel A

Author's Note - Preface: An Invitation to the Feast

> "Come, come, whoever you are. Wanderer, worshiper, lover of leaving. It doesn't matter. Ours is not a caravan of despair. Come, even if you have broken your vows a thousand times. Come, yet again, come, come." – Rumi (Rumi, The Essential Rumi).

Dear seeker of wisdom, lover of beauty, friend of the soul,

You hold in your hands not merely a book, but a key—a key to a treasure chest of celestial jewels, a key to the very chambers of your own heart. For to enter the world of Jalaluddin Rumi is to embark on a journey of self-discovery, a pilgrimage to the center of being, a love affair with the Divine that has no end.

As you open these pages, imagine yourself standing at the threshold of a grand feast hall. The air is thick with the scent of rose water and incense, the sound of a distant new flute beckons you forward. This feast is not one of mere physical sustenance, but a banquet for the soul, where each morsel is a taste of divine wisdom, each sip a draught of cosmic love.

Rumi, our host for this grand occasion, lived and wrote in the 13th century, yet his words resonate with an immediacy that transcends time and culture. Born in what is now Afghanistan and eventually settling in Konya, Turkey, Rumi's life was a testament to the transformative power of love. A respected scholar and teacher, his encounter with the wandering dervish Shams of Tabriz set his soul ablaze, igniting a fire of divine passion that would produce some of the most sublime poetry the world has ever known.

In these pages, you will find not only the life story of this remarkable man, but an invitation to awaken to the extraordinary that pulses within the ordinary moments of your own life. Rumi's words are not relics of a distant past, but living waters that continue to nourish the seeds of awakening in all who drink from their depths. As you read, you may find that Rumi is not speaking to you across the centuries, but whispering directly into your heart, here and now.

Consider this book as a mirror, carefully crafted to reflect not just Rumi's wisdom, but your own innate knowing. Each chapter, each poem, each contemplative exercise is designed to turn you gently towards your own inner light. For as Rumi reminds us (Schimmel, A. 1992):
"Why do you stay in prison when the door is so wide open? Move outside the tangle of fear-thinking. Live in silence."
As you explore these chapters, allow yourself to be more than a passive

reader. Let Rumi's poetry wash over you like waves upon the shore of your consciousness, slowly eroding the hardened beliefs and habitual patterns that keep you separate from the vast ocean of being. Let his wisdom challenge you, comfort you, and ultimately transform you.

Imagine each verse as a key, unlocking doors within your own psyche that you perhaps didn't even know existed. Behind one door, you might find a garden of sensual delight, where every flower is a testament to divine beauty. Behind another, a tavern where the wine of spiritual intoxication flows freely, inviting you to lose yourself in ecstatic union with the Beloved. Yet another might open onto a battlefield, where you're called to confront your own shadows, to wrestle with the very angels of your nature.

We will delve into Rumi's biography, not as dry historical fact, but as a mythic journey that mirrors our own quest for meaning and connection. From his early years as a respected scholar to his transformative encounter with Shams, from the agony of separation to the ecstasy of union, Rumi's life offers a roadmap for our own spiritual unfolding. As you read, consider:

- Where are you on your own spiritual journey?

- What are the Shams in your life—the catalyst that might set your soul ablaze?

- How might you open yourself to a love so vast it consumes everything in its path?

We will explore the themes that weave through his poetry—divine love, spiritual longing, the alchemy of suffering, the dance of opposites—not as abstract concepts, but as lived realities that can illuminate our own path. Each theme is a facet of the diamond of spiritual awakening, reflecting different aspects of the one great truth that Rumi points us towards.

Take, for instance, the theme of divine love. For Rumi, love is not merely a human emotion, but the very fabric of the cosmos, the force that moves the sun and stars. He writes (Rumi, The Essential Rumi):

"Your task is not to seek for love, but merely to seek and find all the barriers within yourself that you have built against it."

As you contemplate these words, consider:

- What barriers have you built against love in your own life?

- How might you begin to dismantle them?

- What would it mean to live as if love were the fundamental reality of existence?

Or consider the theme of spiritual longing. Rumi often speaks of the pain of separation from the Divine as a kind of exquisite wound, a necessary stage in the journey towards union. He tells us (Rumi, The Essential Rumi):

"The wound is the place where the Light enters you."

Reflect on this paradox:

- What wounds in your own life might be openings for divine light?

- How might you reframe your suffering as an opportunity for growth and illumination?

- What would it mean to welcome even your pain as a beloved guest?

In the treasury of Rumi's poetry that forms the heart of this book, you will find freshly translated verses that seek to capture not just the literal meaning of his words, but the ecstatic spirit that animates them. Each poem is an invitation to taste the wine of divine intoxication, to whirl in the dance of cosmic love, to lose yourself in order to find your truest self.

As you read these poems, allow yourself to become intoxicated with their beauty and depth. Don't worry if you don't understand every metaphor or allusion. Rumi's poetry is meant to be felt as much as understood, to bypass the rational mind and speak directly to the heart. Let the rhythms of his words become the beating of your own heart, let his images paint themselves across the canvas of your imagination.

For instance, when you encounter these lines (Rumi, The Essential Rumi):
"Out beyond ideas of wrongdoing and right doing,
there is a field. I'll meet you there.
When the soul lies down in that grass,
the world is too full to talk about."

Don't just read them, but enter into them. Imagine yourself stepping into that field beyond judgment, feel the grass beneath your feet, the vastness of the sky above. What does it feel like to let go of all your preconceptions, to meet reality naked and undefended?

Or consider this verse (Rumi, The Essential Rumi):
"You were born with potential.
You were born with goodness and trust.
You were born with ideals and dreams.
You were born with greatness.
You were born with wings.
You are not meant for crawling, so don't.
You have wings.
Learn to use them and fly."

As you read, feel those wings unfurling within you. What dreams and potentials have you left dormant? What would it mean to spread your wings and soar?

But this book is not content to let Rumi's wisdom remain on the page. Throughout our journey, you will find contemplative exercises, reflection questions, and invitations to embody Rumi's teachings in your daily life. For as Rumi himself reminds us (Rumi, The Essential Rumi):
"There is a candle in your heart, ready to be kindled.
There is a void in your soul, ready to be filled.
You feel it, don't you?"

These exercises are designed to kindle that candle, to fill that void, to bring Rumi's teachings to life in your own experience. They range from simple meditation practices to more elaborate visualizations, from journaling prompts to interpersonal exercises.

For example, you might be invited to:

- Spend a day speaking only in poetry, allowing your words to rise from a deeper place than your ordinary mind.

- Practice seeing the face of the Beloved in every person you encounter, treating each interaction as a divine rendezvous.

- Write a love letter to your own soul, acknowledging its beauty and potential.

- Engage in a whirling meditation, allowing your body to become a living prayer.

- Seek out your own Shams—a person, place, or experience that ignites your passion and calls you to a deeper level of being.

These are not mere intellectual exercises, but invitations to lived experience. For Rumi's wisdom is not meant to be merely understood, but embodied. As he tells us:

"There is a way between voice and presence where information flows.
In disciplined silence it opens.
With wandering talk it closes."

So as you engage with these practices, allow yourself to enter into that space between voice and presence. Let the information flow not just into your mind, but into your heart, your body, your very being.

This journey we're embarking on is not a linear path, but a spiral dance. We'll circle around key themes and ideas, viewing them from different angles, allowing their wisdom to seep into us gradually. Don't be surprised if you find yourself returning to certain poems or practices again and again, each time discovering new layers of meaning.

And remember, this is not a journey to be rushed. Take your time with each chapter, each poem, each exercise. Allow the wisdom to marinate, to work its subtle alchemy within you. As Rumi reminds us:

"Patience is not sitting and waiting, it is foreseeing. It is looking at the thorn and seeing the rose, looking at the night and seeing the day. Lovers are patient and know that the moon needs time to become full."

So be patient with yourself, with the process. Trust that the seeds we're planting together will bloom in their own time.

As we embark on this journey together, it's important to acknowledge that Rumi's path is not always an easy one. He calls us to a radical honesty, a fierce devotion, a willingness to be broken open by love. He tells us (Rumi: The Book of Love):

"Your task is not to seek for love, but merely to seek and find all the barriers within yourself that you have built against it."

This means facing our shadows, confronting our fears, letting go of our most cherished illusions. It means being willing to be transformed, to die to our small self in order to be reborn in the vastness of divine love.

But Rumi also assures us that the reward is worth the risk. He promises us nothing less than union with the Beloved, a love so vast it encompasses all of existence. He invites us to (Rumi: The Big Red Book):

"Close both eyes to see with the other eye."

So as we begin, I invite you to close your outer eyes for a moment. Take a deep breath, and with your inner eye, see yourself stepping into Rumi's feast hall. Feel the plush carpet beneath your feet, smell the fragrant incense, hear the distant strains of music. See Rumi himself, eyes twinkling with divine mischief, hand outstretched in welcome.

For make no mistake, this book is more than just a collection of words on a page. It is a living invitation, a summons to awakening, a love letter from the heart of existence to your own soul.

So come, dear friend. Let us light that candle together. Let us fill that void with the boundless love that Rumi points us towards. Let us feast on the wisdom of a master who understood that the deepest truths can only be approached through the language of the heart.

Turn the page, and let our journey begin. For as Rumi tells us (Rumi: The Essential Rumi):

"Start a huge, foolish project, like Noah...it makes absolutely no difference what people think of you."

This book, this journey we're embarking on together, is just such a foolish project. It's a project of opening our hearts, of expanding our consciousness, of remembering our essential oneness with all that is.

Are you ready? Take a deep breath, open your heart, and step into the feast hall of Rumi's wisdom. The table is set, the wine is poured, and the Beloved awaits. Let the journey begin.

Introduction: Mystic Rumination - The Enduring Flame of Rumi's Love
Mystic Rumination:

Mystic rumination refers to a deep, contemplative practice often associated with mystical or spiritual experiences. It involves intense focus and reflection on profound or esoteric subjects, often leading to spiritual insights or enlightenment. This practice is common in various religious and spiritual traditions, where practitioners seek to connect with the divine or gain a deeper understanding of the nature of existence.

Key Aspects:

1. Deep Contemplation:

- Engages in prolonged, intense thought or meditation on spiritual or mystical subjects.

2. Spiritual Insight:

- Aims to attain deeper understanding, enlightenment, or connection with the divine.

3. Tradition-Specific Practices:

- Varies across different religious and spiritual traditions, such as Sufi meditation, Christian mysticism, or Buddhist contemplation.

4. Inner Experience:

- Focuses on the internal experience, often involving visions, profound thoughts, or a sense of unity with the universe.

5. Purpose:

- Seeks to transcend ordinary reality and achieve a higher state of consciousness or spiritual awakening.

Benefits:
- Enhanced spiritual understanding.
- Greater inner peace and mental clarity.
- Connection with a higher power or the universe.
- Insights into the nature of existence and the self.

Mystic rumination is a profound practice aimed at exploring the deeper, often hidden aspects of spirituality and existence, offering practitioners a path to transcendental experiences and enlightenment.

In the vast constellation of mystical poets, few stars shine as brightly or as enduringly as Jalaluddin Rumi. Born in 13th century Persia, his words continue to ignite hearts and illuminate minds across cultures and centuries. But what is it about Rumi that speaks so powerfully to our modern condition? Why, in an age of unprecedented scientific knowledge and technological advancement, do we find ourselves increasingly drawn to the ecstatic utterances of a medieval Sufi mystic?

Perhaps it is because Rumi's poetry touches something timeless within us, a longing that transcends the boundaries of culture, religion, and even time itself. In a world that often feels fragmented and alienating, Rumi offers us a vision of radical unity (Rumi: The Masnavi, Book One):

"I am not of the East, nor of the West, nor of the land, nor of the sea;

I am not of Nature's mint, nor of the circling heavens.

I am not of earth, nor of water, nor of air, nor of fire;

I am not of the empyrean, nor of the dust, nor of existence, nor of entity.

I am not of India, nor of China, nor of Bulgaria, nor of Saqsin;

I am not of the kingdom of Iraq, nor of the country of Khorasan.

I am not of this world, nor of the next, nor of Paradise, nor of Hell;

I am not of Adam, nor of Eve, nor of Eden and Rizwan.

My place is the Placeless, my trace is the Traceless;

'Tis neither body nor soul, for I belong to the soul of the Beloved."

In these lines, we encounter the heart of Rumi's message – that beneath the surface differences that seem to divide us, there is a deeper unity, a shared essence that connects all beings. This is not a philosophical abstraction for Rumi, but a lived reality, a state of being that he invites us to experience for ourselves.

Throughout this book, we will explore the many facets of Rumi's wisdom, from his teachings on love and longing to his insights into the nature of consciousness and the cosmos. We will trace the arc of his life, from his early years as a respected scholar to the transformative encounter with his spiritual friend and teacher, Shams of Tabriz, that set his soul ablaze and gave birth to some of the most sublime poetry ever penned.

But more than just an exploration of Rumi's life and work, this book is an invitation to a way of being. Rumi's words are not meant to be merely read and admired, but to be lived, to be embodied. As he tells us (Rumi: The Essential Rumi):

"Don't be satisfied with stories, how things have gone with others. Unfold your own myth."

As we embark on this journey together, let us approach Rumi's words with both reverence and playfulness, with the mind of a scholar and the heart of a lover. For Rumi himself was both – a learned man of profound intellect and a passionate mystic intoxicated with divine love. He invites us to bring our whole selves to this exploration, to engage not just with our minds, but with our hearts, our bodies, our very souls.

"Come, come, whoever you are.
Wanderer, worshiper, lover of leaving.
It doesn't matter.
Ours is not a caravan of despair.
Come, even if you have broken your vows a thousand times.
Come, yet again, come, come."

With these words, Rumi extends an invitation to all of us – regardless of our background, our beliefs, or our past mistakes. It is in this spirit of radical inclusivity and boundless love that we begin our journey into the heart of Rumi's wisdom.

As we embark on this journey through the wisdom of Rumi, we find ourselves standing at the threshold of a vast spiritual landscape. Jalaluddin Rumi, the 13th-century Persian poet and mystic, continues to captivate hearts and minds across cultures and centuries. His words, at once intimate and cosmic, invite us into a world where the boundaries between the human and the divine blur, where every atom dances with the energy of love.

Rumi's life story reads like a spiritual epic. Born in 1207 in Balkh (present-day Afghanistan), he fled the Mongol invasion with his family, eventually settling in Konya, Turkey. It was here, at the age of 37, that Rumi encountered the wandering dervish Shams of Tabriz—a meeting that would ignite the flame of divine love in Rumi's heart and transform him from a respected scholar into an ecstatic poet of love.

The significance of Rumi's work in our modern world cannot be overstated. In an age often characterized by materialism, division, and spiritual hunger, Rumi's poetry offers a balm for the soul and a bridge between cultures. His verses speak to the universal human longing for connection, meaning, and transcendence. As Coleman Barks, one of Rumi's most popular translators, notes,

"Rumi is able to verbalize the highly personal and often confusing world of personal growth and development in a very clear and direct fashion. He does not offend anyone, and he includes everyone" (Barks, "The Essential Rumi," 1995).

In "Mystic Ruminations," we aim to explore the multifaceted jewel of Rumi's wisdom, examining how his teachings on love, longing, surrender, and unity can illuminate our own spiritual paths. This book is not merely an academic study or a collection of beautiful verses; it is an invitation to engage in a living dialogue with Rumi's words, to allow them to penetrate our hearts and transform our lives.

We will delve into the art of spiritual divine flirtation—the playful yet profound dance between the human and the divine that characterizes much of Rumi's poetry. We'll explore the themes of love and longing, surrender and ecstasy, paradox and universality that run like golden threads through his work. Along the way, we'll engage in enchanted conversations—with Rumi's poetry, with contemporary thinkers, and with our own deepest selves.

As we journey through these pages, may we approach Rumi's wisdom with both the rigor of scholars and the open hearts of lovers. For as Rumi himself reminds us:

"The time has come to turn your heart into a temple of fire.

Your essence is gold hidden in dust.

To reveal its splendor, you need to burn in the fire of love."

So come, let us step into the circle of lovers and allow the whirling dance to begin. May Rumi's timeless wisdom guide us to a deeper understanding of love, unity, and the divine connection within. This volume is your invitation to awakening, urging you to embrace the present moment and the boundless love that resides within us all.

Part I: The Life and Legacy of Rumi

Chapter 1: From Balkh to Konya: The Making of a Mystic

The story of Rumi begins not with his birth, but with a journey. In the year 1215, as the Mongol armies swept across Central Asia, a caravan set out from the city of Balkh in what is now Afghanistan. Among the travelers was a family of scholars and mystics – Bahauddin Valad, his wife, and their young son, Jalaluddin. This boy, not yet ten years old, would grow to become the poet and mystic we know as Rumi. When Rumi was about eight years old, his family was forced to leave Balkh due to the impending Mongol invasion. This departure marked the beginning of a long journey that would take the young Rumi across the Islamic world, exposing him to diverse cultures and intellectual traditions.

The experience of displacement and the uncertainty of travel would later find expression in Rumi's poetry, which often uses the metaphor of journey to describe the spiritual quest:

"The breeze at dawn has secrets to tell you. Don't go back to sleep."

Rumi's father, Baha ud-Din Walad, known as "Sultan of the Scholars," was a renowned theologian and Sufi master. His mother, Mu'mina Khatun, was said to be a descendant of the Prophet Muhammad. From his earliest years, Rumi was immersed in an atmosphere of spiritual seeking and intellectual rigor that would shape his future path.

Balkh, at the time of Rumi's birth in 1207, was a center of learning and culture, often called "the mother of cities." It was a crucible of diverse influences – Persian, Arabic, Turkish, and Indian – that would shape the young Jalaluddin's worldview. His father, Bahauddin, known as the "Sultan of the Scholars," was a respected theologian and Sufi master. From his earliest years, Jalaluddin was immersed in an atmosphere of spiritual seeking and intellectual rigor.

The intellectual climate of Balkh was characterized by a vibrant interplay between different schools of Islamic thought, as well as engagement with Greek philosophy and pre-Islamic Persian wisdom traditions. This rich tapestry of ideas would later be reflected in the vast scope of Rumi's own writings.

The family's journey westward was more than a physical migration; it was a spiritual pilgrimage that would take them through Persia, Arabia, and eventually to Anatolia. Along the way, young Jalaluddin absorbed the sights, sounds, and wisdom of the lands they passed through. In Baghdad, it is said, the aging Sufi master Attar recognized the boy's potential, declaring,

"Soon this son of yours will set the spiritual aspirants of this world afire."

After years of travel, the family finally settled in Konya, in present-day Turkey. It was here, in this cosmopolitan city at the crossroads of East and West, that Jalaluddin would come of age, inherit his father's position as a religious teacher, and eventually undergo the transformation that would turn him into the ecstatic poet we know as Rumi.

In Konya, Jalaluddin quickly distinguished himself as a brilliant scholar and charismatic teacher. He mastered not only Islamic law and theology but also the secular sciences of his day. By his early thirties, he had become a respected figure in the intellectual and spiritual life of the city, with hundreds of students seeking his guidance.

It was in Konya, at the age of 37, that Rumi encountered the wandering dervish Shams of Tabriz—a meeting that would ignite the flame of divine love in Rumi's heart and transform him from a respected scholar into an ecstatic poet of love. This pivotal encounter set the stage for Rumi's profound spiritual awakening and the outpouring of mystical poetry that would follow. By his early thirties, Rumi had become a respected figure in the intellectual and spiritual life of Konya, with hundreds of students seeking his guidance. His lectures were said to be electrifying, weaving together Quranic exegesis, mystical insights, and practical guidance for daily life.

Yet for all his learning and acclaim, there was a restlessness in Rumi's soul, a sense that something essential was missing. He would later write:

"I was looking for myself
but I was not in the house.
I was knocking at my own door,
but I was outside."

This feeling of incompleteness, this intuition of a greater truth beyond the reach of ordinary knowledge, is a recurring theme in the lives of mystics across traditions. For Rumi, it set the stage for the cataclysmic encounter that would shatter his world and remake him into a poet of divine love.

But before we come to that pivotal moment, let us pause to consider the world that shaped the young Rumi. 13th century Anatolia was a place of great cultural ferment and spiritual diversity. Christians, Jews, and Muslims lived side by side, often engaging in deep philosophical and theological debates. Sufi orders were flourishing, offering a more direct and experiential approach to spirituality than the sometimes rigid orthodoxies of established religion.

In this environment, Rumi's early teachings already showed signs of the expansive, inclusive spirituality that would later characterize his poetry. He drew not only on Islamic sources but on a wide range of wisdom traditions. His lectures were said to be electrifying, weaving together Quranic exegesis, mystical insights, and practical guidance for daily life.

Yet for all his eloquence and wisdom, Rumi would later say of this period:

"I was a scholar.

They made me a teacher.

But I was really just a lover

in disguise."

It would take a dramatic encounter to strip away that disguise and reveal the lover at the core of Rumi's being. That encounter was waiting just around the corner, in the form of a wandering dervish named Shams of Tabriz.

As we stand on the cusp of this transformative meeting, we can see in Rumi's early life the seeds of what was to come – the deep spirituality inherited from his father, the vast learning acquired through years of study, the openness to diverse influences, and the restless seeking for a truth beyond words. All of these elements would be thrown into the alchemical fire ignited by his meeting with Shams, emerging transformed into the pure gold of Rumi's poetry.

In the realm of spiritual literature, few concepts are as intriguing and potentially misunderstood as that of divine flirtation. Yet, in Rumi's poetry, we find a master of this delicate art, one who dances on the knife-edge between the sacred and the sensual, the cosmic and the intimate.

Spiritual flirtation, as embodied in Rumi's work, is not a trivial or disrespectful act. Rather, it is a way of engaging with the divine that is at once playful and profound, tender and fierce. It is an approach to the sacred that recognizes the element of mystery and delight inherent in the spiritual journey.

As scholar William C. Chittick notes in "The Sufi Path of Love: The Spiritual Teachings of Rumi" (1983), "Rumi's poetry is characterized by a constant tension between presence and absence, union and separation. This dynamic interplay creates a sense of divine flirtation—a push and pull between

25

the lover and the Beloved that keeps the spiritual seeker in a state of passionate alertness."

Consider these lines from Rumi:

"I am a sculptor, a molder of form.
In every moment I shape an idol.
But then, in front of you, I melt them down
I can rouse a hundred forms
and fill them with spirit,
but when I look into your face,
I want to throw them in the fire."

Here, we see the essence of spiritual flirtation. The poet creates beautiful forms—ideas, concepts, even religious practices—only to dissolve them in the presence of the divine. This playful creation and destruction mirrors the cosmic dance of manifestation and dissolution, inviting us to hold our spiritual constructs lightly, always ready to melt them in the fire of direct experience.

Rumi's use of sensual imagery to describe the spiritual journey is another aspect of this divine flirtation. He often portrays God as a seductive lover, employing the language of earthly passion to convey the intensity of spiritual longing (Rumi, The Essential Rumi):

"The minute I heard my first love story,
I started looking for you, not knowing
how blind that was.
Lovers don't finally meet somewhere.
They're in each other all along."

This blending of the sensual and the spiritual serves multiple purposes. It makes the abstract concept of divine love more tangible and relatable to human experience. It also challenges our tendency to compartmentalize the sacred and the profane, inviting us to see the divine presence in all aspects of life.

Moreover, Rumi's spiritual flirtation embodies a core principle of Sufi philosophy—the idea that love, in all its forms, is a bridge to divine love. As he writes (Rumi, The Essential Rumi):

"Love is the bridge between you and everything."

By engaging in this divine flirtation, Rumi invites us to approach our spiritual path with a sense of joy, wonder, and passionate engagement. He encourages us to be bold in our approach to the divine, to woo and be wooed by the cosmos itself.

Yet, this flirtation is not without its challenges. Rumi often speaks of the pain of separation, the burning longing for union with the divine. This too is part of the flirtation—the exquisite tension between presence and absence, between the glimpse of divine beauty and the ache of apparent separation (Rumi, The Essential Rumi).

"The wound is the place where the Light enters you."

In these words, Rumi transforms even our spiritual struggles into part of the divine romance, seeing our very woundedness as an opening for grace.

As we explore Rumi's art of spiritual flirtation, we are invited to bring more playfulness, passion, and wonder to our own spiritual lives. We are challenged to engage with the divine not just through solemn ritual or abstract philosophy, but through a living, breathing relationship full of surprise, delight, and transformative power.

In the chapters that follow, we will delve deeper into the various facets of this divine flirtation—the interplay of love and longing, the ecstasy of surrender, the embrace of paradox, and the recognition of the divine in all things. Through it all, may we cultivate the art of spiritual flirtation in our own lives, learning to dance with the divine in a way that is both lighthearted and profound, both intimate and cosmic.

As Rumi reminds us (Rumi: The Essential Rumi):

"Let the beauty we love be what we do.

There are hundreds of ways to kneel and kiss the ground."

May we find our own beautiful ways to kneel and kiss the ground, to engage in this eternal dance of divine flirtation.

In the next chapter, we will explore this pivotal encounter and the revolution it sparked in Rumi's life and work. But for now, let us sit with the image of Rumi on the eve of this great change – a respected scholar and teacher, outwardly accomplished but inwardly yearning, not yet knowing that he stood on the threshold of a love that would consume him entirely and give birth to some of the most sublime poetry the world has ever known.

The Reed Flute's Song

Listen to the reed and the tale it tells,
How it sings of separation:
Ever since they cut me from the reed bed,
My wail has caused men and women to weep.
I want a heart torn open with longing
So that I might relate the pain of love.
Whoever has been parted from his source
Longs to return to that state of union.
At every gathering I play my lament.
I'm a friend to both happy and sad.
Each befriended me for his own reasons,
Yet none searched out the secrets I contain.
My secret is not far from my lament,
Yet it is not visible to the eye.
The body is not hidden from the soul,
Nor is the soul hidden from the body,
Yet the soul is not for everyone to see.

Chapter 2: The Shams Revolution: Love Sets Rumi Ablaze

Before we delve into the transformative meeting between Rumi and Shams, it's crucial to understand who Shams of Tabriz was. Unlike Rumi, who was a respected scholar and teacher, Shams was a wandering dervish, known for his unconventional behavior and provocative spiritual teachings.

Shams hailed from Tabriz, a city in northwestern Iran known for its rich cultural and mystical traditions. Little is known about his early life, but accounts describe him as a man of fierce intensity, profound spiritual insight, and a disregard for social conventions. He was said to have traveled widely, seeking a spiritual companion who could match his own depth of understanding.

On a crisp autumn day in 1244, the streets of Konya witnessed an encounter that would change the course of mystical literature forever. Jalaluddin Rumi, the respected scholar and teacher, met Shams of Tabriz, a wandering dervish with eyes that burned with divine fire. The details of their first meeting are shrouded in legend, but the impact was undeniable and immediate.

One version of the story tells us that Shams approached Rumi as he sat by a fountain, surrounded by books. Shams asked him, "What are you doing?" Rumi replied, "This is called knowledge, something you are unaware of." Shams then tossed Rumi's precious books into the water. Aghast, Rumi rescued them, only to find them completely dry.

"This is called knowledge," Shams said, "something you are unaware of."

Whether this exchange happened literally or symbolically, it captures the essence of what Shams brought into Rumi's life – a direct, experiential knowledge that transcended book learning and rational thought. Shams awakened in Rumi a dimension of being that had lain dormant, hidden beneath layers of scholarly erudition.

Rumi himself described the transformative power of this encounter:
> "What I once thought of as God
> I met today in a human being."

From the moment of their meeting, Rumi and Shams became inseparable.

They retreated into long periods of seclusion, engaging in deep spiritual conversations that often lasted for days. These conversations, or sohbet, were more than intellectual exchanges; they were a kind of alchemical process, transforming both participants at the deepest level.

For Rumi, this period marked a profound shift. The respected scholar who had once delivered formal sermons now began to sing and dance in the streets. He neglected his teaching duties, scandalized some of his more conservative followers, and poured all his energy into the intoxicating presence of Shams.

In Shams, Rumi had found both a mirror and a window – a reflection of his own deepest nature and an opening to the divine. He wrote:

"I was dead, I came alive.
I was tears, I became laughter.
Love's power entered me,
and I became everlasting power."

But this period of ecstatic communion was not to last. After about two years, Shams disappeared as suddenly as he had arrived. Some accounts suggest he was murdered by Rumi's jealous disciples or family members. Others say he simply moved on, his work of awakening Rumi complete.

Whatever the truth, Shams' departure plunged Rumi into a period of intense grief and longing. It was out of this anguish that his poetry began to flow. What had been ignited in Rumi during his time with Shams now found expression in an outpouring of lyrical verse that would continue for the rest of his life.

In his grief, Rumi discovered that Shams was not separate from him, but a manifestation of the divine beloved that dwells within all hearts:

"Why should I seek? I am the same as He.
His essence speaks through me.
I have been looking for myself!"

This realization marked the birth of Rumi as we know him – the ecstatic poet whose verses sing of the pain of separation and the joy of union, the seeker who finds the beloved in every face, the mystic who recognizes that lover and beloved are ultimately one.

The collection of poems that emerged from this period, known as the Divan-e Shams-e Tabrizi, is a testament to the transformative power of divine love. In these verses, we find Rumi wrestling with the mystery of existence, celebrating the beauty of creation, and always, always pointing towards the ineffable reality that lies beyond words (Rumi, The Essential Rumi):

"Silence is the language of God,

all else is poor translation."

Yet paradoxically, it is through Rumi's words that countless seekers have found their way to that divine silence. His poetry became a bridge between worlds, inviting readers to taste the wine of spiritual intoxication for themselves.

The Shams revolution in Rumi's life teaches us that true transformation often comes through encounter – with a teacher, a friend, or an aspect of ourselves that we have long denied. It reminds us that the path to awakening is not always smooth or socially acceptable, that it might require us to break out of old patterns and risk everything for the sake of truth.

Most importantly, Rumi's experience with Shams shows us that the beloved we seek is not separate from us. The fire that Shams ignited in Rumi was Rumi's own divine nature, waiting to be recognized and expressed.

As we contemplate this pivotal period in Rumi's life, we might ask ourselves: Who or what plays the role of Shams in our own lives? What encounters have shaken us out of complacency and opened us to new dimensions of being? How might we, like Rumi, allow our pain to become a portal to greater love and understanding?

In the vast ocean of Rumi's poetry, no themes are more prevalent or powerful than those of love and longing. These twin forces form the very heartbeat of his work, pulsing through every line with an intensity that continues to resonate across centuries and cultures.

For Rumi, love is not merely a human emotion or a romantic ideal. It is the very essence of existence, the force that moves the cosmos and animates all of creation. As he declares:

"Love is the water of life. And a lover is a soul of fire!

The universe turns differently when fire loves water."

This cosmic vision of love infuses all of Rumi's work, elevating even the most intimate expressions of human affection to the level of divine communion. In Rumi's world, every act of love becomes a participation in the eternal dance of creation.

Yet, hand in hand with this exalted vision of love comes the experience of longing. In the Sufi tradition, this spiritual yearning is known as "ishq," a consuming passion for the divine that both wounds and heals the soul. Rumi gives voice to this longing in countless poems (Rumi, The Essential Rumi):

"There is a candle in your heart, ready to be kindled.

There is a void in your soul, ready to be filled.

You feel it, don't you?"

This longing, far from being a source of suffering to be eliminated, is celebrated by Rumi as the very engine of spiritual growth. It is the force that propels the seeker on their journey, the "pain of separation" that paradoxically leads to union.

As scholar Annemarie Schimmel notes in her seminal work "The Triumphal Sun: A Study of the Works of Jalaloddin Rumi" (1978), "For Rumi, longing is not a state to be overcome, but a divine gift that keeps the lover in constant movement towards the Beloved. It is the very spark of spiritual life."

Rumi often employs powerful metaphors to convey the interplay of love and longing. One of the most famous is that of the reed flute, separated from its reed bed:

"Listen to the story told by the reed,

of being separated.

Since I was cut from the reedbed,

I have made this crying sound."

The reed flute becomes a symbol of the human soul, its haunting music born from the pain of separation from its divine source. Yet this very separation is what allows it to make music—just as our sense of separation from the divine is what fuels our spiritual journey.

Another recurring metaphor in Rumi's poetry is that of intoxication. He often speaks of love as a kind of divine wine that inebriates the soul:

"Drink wine. This is life eternal. This is all that youth will give you.

It is the season for wine, roses and drunken friends. Be happy for this moment.

This moment is your life."

This imagery of intoxication serves multiple purposes. It conveys the ecstatic nature of divine love, which transcends ordinary consciousness. It also challenges conventional notions of sobriety and intoxication, suggesting that true sobriety lies in losing oneself in divine love, while attachment to the material world is a form of intoxication.

Rumi's treatment of love and longing is not confined to the spiritual realm. He also writes powerfully about human love, seeing it as a reflection and a portal to divine love (Rumi, The Essential Rumi):

"The minute I heard my first love story,
I started looking for you, not knowing
how blind that was.
Lovers don't finally meet somewhere.
They're in each other all along."

Here, Rumi suggests that the search for human love is ultimately a search for the divine beloved who dwells within us. This perspective transforms every act of human love into a sacred encounter, a glimpse of the divine in the eyes of the other.

Yet Rumi is also keenly aware of the pain that often accompanies love. He writes of heartbreak and loss with profound empathy, always finding in these experiences an opportunity for spiritual growth (Rumi, The Essential Rumi):

"The wound is the place where the Light enters you."

In Rumi's vision, even the pain of love becomes a doorway to greater union, a breaking open of the heart that allows more divine light to enter.

As we contemplate Rumi's teachings on love and longing, we are invited to examine our own experiences of these powerful forces. How might our understanding of love expand if we viewed it through Rumi's cosmic lens? How might we embrace our longings—even our pain—as fuel for spiritual growth?

Rumi's teachings on love, unity, inner peace, and the divine connection within us all remain profoundly relevant in our contemporary world. His emphasis on the interconnectedness of all beings offers a spiritual foundation for addressing global challenges like environmental crisis and social inequality. His focus on inner transformation provides a counterbalance to the materialistic tendencies of our age.

In a world often divided by religious and cultural differences, Rumi's universal message is perhaps more relevant than ever. It offers a vision of spirituality that is both deeply rooted and radically inclusive, that honors tradition while transcending its boundaries.

Rumi challenges us to dive deep into the ocean of love, to allow ourselves to be consumed by divine longing. For it is in this consuming fire, he suggests, that we find our true selves and our ultimate union with the divine.

As we continue our journey through "Mystic Ruminations," may we carry with us Rumi's passionate vision of love and longing. May we learn to see all our experiences of love—human and divine, joyful and painful—as part of the great cosmic dance of reunion with the Beloved.

In Rumi's immortal words (Rumi, The Essential Rumi):

"Your task is not to seek for love,

but merely to seek and find all the barriers within yourself

that you have built against it."

May we have the courage to seek out and dissolve these barriers, opening ourselves fully to the transformative power of love and longing.

In the next chapter, we will explore how Rumi integrated this profound awakening into the remainder of his life, becoming the "whirling dervish" whose influence continues to spread across the globe. But for now, let us sit with the image of Rumi in the throes of divine passion, newly awakened to the love that permeates all existence, his heart an open wound from which pours the sweet wine of mystical poetry.

The Guest House

This being human is a guest house.
Every morning a new arrival.
A joy, a depression, a meanness,
some momentary awareness comes
as an unexpected visitor.
Welcome and entertain them all!
Even if they're a crowd of sorrows,
who violently sweep your house
empty of its furniture,
still, treat each guest honorably.
He may be clearing you out
for some new delight.
The dark thought, the shame, the malice,
meet them at the door laughing,
and invite them in.
Be grateful for whoever comes,
because each has been sent
as a guide from beyond.

This poem beautifully encapsulates Rumi's teachings on embracing all experiences - including love, longing, joy, and sorrow - as opportunities for spiritual growth and transformation. It aligns perfectly with the chapter's exploration of how Rumi's encounter with Shams led to a profound awakening, and how he came to see even pain and separation as pathways to greater union with the divine.

Chapter 3: The Whirling Dervish: Rumi's Later Years and Lasting Impact

The disappearance of Shams marked the end of one chapter in Rumi's life, but it was far from the end of his spiritual journey. In the years that followed, Rumi would integrate the fire of awakening kindled by Shams into a new way of being and teaching that would touch countless lives, both in his own time and for centuries to come.

After a period of intense grief and searching for Shams, Rumi gradually came to realize that the presence he sought was not to be found in the outer world, but within his own heart. He wrote:

"Why should I seek? I am the same as He.

His essence speaks through me.

I have been looking for myself!"

This realization marked a new phase in Rumi's life. No longer the formal religious teacher, nor the love-mad seeker, Rumi emerged as a poet-saint whose words and actions embodied the union of human and divine love.

It was during this period that Rumi began the practice that would become synonymous with his name: the meditative whirling dance known as sama. Legend has it that Rumi was walking through the marketplace one day when he heard the rhythmic hammering of the goldsmiths. In the repetitive sound, he heard the name of God - "Allah, Allah, Allah" - and began to turn in ecstatic revolution.

This spontaneous expression of spiritual ecstasy evolved into a formal practice, which Rumi often engaged in with his followers. The whirling dance became a physical enactment of Rumi's central teaching: that by emptying ourselves of ego, we can become vessels for divine love to flow through. As he put it:

"We come spinning out of nothingness,

scattering stars like dust.

The stars form a circle,

and in the center, we dance."

During this period, Rumi's poetic output was prodigious. In addition to continuing to compose ghazals (lyric poems) that were collected in the Divan-e

Shams-e Tabrizi, he began work on his masterpiece, the Masnavi. This monumental work, comprising six books of spiritual teachings in the form of stories, parables, and mystical insights, has been called "the Quran in Persian" for its profound impact on Islamic spirituality.

In the Divan, Rumi often speaks in the voice of Shams, blurring the lines between lover and beloved, seeker and sought. This work is a testament to the enduring impact of Shams on Rumi's spiritual and poetic vision.

The Masnavi defies easy categorization. It is at once a guide to spiritual practice, a compendium of Sufi wisdom, a critique of religious hypocrisy, and a celebration of divine love. Throughout its thousands of verses, Rumi returns again and again to the central theme of his teaching: the transformative power of love. He writes (Rumi, The Essential Rumi):

"Your task is not to seek for love,
but merely to seek and find all the barriers within yourself
that you have built against it."

Even as his fame grew, Rumi remained committed to the path of humility and service. He established a Sufi order, the Mevlevi, which continues to this day. But he was clear that the goal was not to create another sectarian group, but to dissolve the barriers that separate human beings from each other and from God. He taught:

"Not Christian or Jew or Muslim, not Hindu,
Buddhist, Sufi, or Zen. Not any religion
or cultural system. I am not from the East
or the West, not out of the ocean or up
from the ground, not natural or ethereal, not
composed of elements at all. I do not exist,
am not an entity in this world or the next,
did not descend from Adam and Eve or any
origin story. My place is placeless, a trace
of the traceless. Neither body or soul.
I belong to the beloved, have seen the two
worlds as one and that one call to and know,
first, last, outer, inner, only that
breath breathing human being."

Rumi's inclusive vision attracted followers from all walks of life and all religious backgrounds. Christians, Jews, and Muslims alike found in his teachings a path to the heart of their own traditions. This universality would prove to be one of Rumi's most enduring legacies.

As he approached the end of his life, Rumi's teachings took on an increasing urgency. He spoke often of death not as an end, but as a return to the beloved. On December 17, 1273, as he lay on his deathbed, he is said to have recited these lines:

"When you see my corpse being carried

Don't cry for my leaving

I'm not leaving

I'm arriving at eternal love

When you leave me in the grave

Don't say goodbye

Remember a grave is

Only a curtain

For the paradise behind

You'll only see me

Descending into a grave

Now watch me rise

How can there be an end

When the sun sets or

The moon goes down

It looks like the end

It seems like a sunset

But in reality it is a dawn

When the grave locks you up

That is when your soul is freed

Have you ever seen

A seed fallen to earth

Not rise with a new life

Why should you doubt the rise

Of a seed named human

Have you ever seen

A bucket lowered into a well

Coming back empty

Why lament for a soul
When it can come back
Like Joseph from the well
When for the last time
You close your mouth
Your words and soul
Will belong to the world of
No place no time"

Rumi's death was mourned not only by Muslims but by Christians and Jews as well. His funeral procession was said to have lasted 40 days, as people from all faiths came to pay their respects to the man who had taught them to see beyond the boundaries of religion to the unifying force of love.

In the centuries since his death, Rumi's influence has only grown. His poetry has been translated into countless languages and continues to inspire millions around the world. His teachings on love, tolerance, and the unity of all beings remain as relevant today as they were in the 13th century.

Rumi's work has had a profound impact on both Eastern and Western literature and thought. In the Islamic world, he is revered as one of the greatest spiritual masters. In the West, his popularity has soared in recent decades, with his books becoming bestsellers and his quotes widely shared on social media.

The universal appeal of Rumi's message lies in its emphasis on love as the core of spirituality, its celebration of the beauty of creation, and its vision of the fundamental unity of all existence. In a world often divided by religious and cultural differences, Rumi's inclusive spirituality offers a path to harmony and mutual understanding.

As we conclude this overview of Rumi's life, we are left with the image of a man who was continually transforming - from scholar to lover, from grief-stricken seeker to ecstatic poet, from teacher to eternal student of the divine. His life serves as an invitation to each of us to undergo our own transformation, to break free of the limitations we have placed on ourselves, and to whirl in the dance of love that animates the cosmos.

In the chapters that follow, we will delve deeper into the themes and teachings that emerge from Rumi's poetry, exploring how they can illuminate our own spiritual journeys. But for now, let us sit with the eternal wisdom contained in these simple lines (Rumi: The Essential Rumi):

"Let the beauty we love be what we do.
There are hundreds of ways to kneel and kiss the ground."
In the mystical landscape of Rumi's poetry, surrender and ecstasy emerge as twin peaks, intimately connected states that represent the heights of spiritual experience. These themes, central to Sufi practice and philosophy, find their fullest expression in Rumi's impassioned verses.

Surrender, or "taslim" in Arabic, is not a passive resignation in Rumi's work, but an active, loving submission to the divine will. It is the recognition that our limited ego-self is an illusion, and that our true nature is one with the divine. As Rumi puts it:
"You have no need to travel anywhere - journey within yourself.
Enter a mine of rubies and bathe in the splendor of your own light."
This surrender is often portrayed as a kind of death—the death of the false self that paves the way for spiritual rebirth. Rumi famously wrote:
"Die before you die."
Explaining this concept, scholar William C. Chittick writes in "The Sufi Path of Love" (1983),
"For Rumi, to 'die before death' means to realize the illusory nature of the ego and to live from the center of one's true, divine nature. It is the ultimate act of surrender."
This surrender, paradoxically, leads not to loss but to the greatest gain—union with the divine. Rumi uses various metaphors to convey this state of union, often drawing from nature:
"I am a fish. You are the moon.
You cannot touch me, but your light fills the ocean where I live."
Here, the fish represents the individual soul, while the moon symbolizes the divine. The image beautifully captures both the intimacy and the vastness of the soul's relationship with God.

Closely linked to surrender in Rumi's poetry is the concept of ecstasy, or "wajd" in Sufi terminology. This is not mere emotional excitement, but a transcendent state of being where the boundaries of the self-dissolve in the ocean of divine presence. Rumi often describes this state in terms of intoxication:
"Drink wine. This is life eternal. This is all that youth will give you.
It is the season for wine, roses and drunken friends. Be happy for this moment.

This moment is your life."

The imagery of intoxication serves to convey the overwhelming, transformative nature of the ecstatic experience. Just as a drunkard loses their normal inhibitions and self-consciousness, the mystic in a state of ecstasy loses their sense of separate selfhood, merging with the divine beloved.

The practice of sama became central to the Mevlevi Order, a Sufi order founded by Rumi's followers after his death. The Mevlevi dervishes, often called "whirling dervishes" in the West, continue this practice to this day, seeing it as a way to abandon one's nafs (ego) and attain spiritual ecstasy.

Rumi's most famous expression of ecstatic union is perhaps his description of the Sama, or whirling dance, practiced by the Mevlevi order of dervishes he founded (Rumi, The Essential Rumi):

"We came whirling out of nothingness, scattering stars like dust...

The stars made a circle, and in the middle, we dance."

This ecstatic dance becomes a physical embodiment of spiritual surrender and union, with the dervish becoming an empty reed through which the divine breath flows.

Yet Rumi is careful to point out that true ecstasy is not about extraordinary experiences or altered states of consciousness. Rather, it is about fully embracing the present moment, recognizing the divine presence in every aspect of ordinary life:

"Today, like every other day, we wake up empty
and frightened. Don't open the door to the study
and begin reading. Take down a musical instrument.
Let the beauty we love be what we do.
There are hundreds of ways to kneel and kiss the ground."

This perspective transforms every moment into an opportunity for ecstatic union, every action into an act of devotion.

The interplay of surrender and ecstasy in Rumi's work invites us to examine our own spiritual lives. How might we cultivate a deeper surrender in our daily lives? What would it mean to live in a state of constant ecstasy, fully present to the divine in each moment?

Rumi challenges us to move beyond our comfort zones, to let go of our preconceptions and control, and to dive headlong into the ocean of divine love. As he says:

"You have to keep breaking your heart until it opens."

This breaking open is not a destruction, but an expansion—the cracking of the shell that allows the kernel within to grow and flourish.

As we continue our journey through "Mystic Ruminations," may we carry with us Rumi's invitation to surrender and ecstasy. May we learn to dance with abandon in the circle of stars, to lose ourselves in order to find our true selves, and to recognize the extraordinary within the ordinary moments of our lives.

In Rumi's words:

"Gamble everything for love,
if you are a true human being.
If not, leave this gathering.
Half-heartedness doesn't reach into majesty."

These powerful lines encapsulate Rumi's call for total commitment on the spiritual path. For him, surrender is not a halfway measure, but a complete offering of oneself to the divine.

The concept of surrender in Rumi's work is closely tied to the Sufi practice of "fana," or annihilation of the self in God. This state is often described as a "passing away" of individual consciousness into divine consciousness. As Annemarie Schimmel notes in "Mystical Dimensions of Islam" (1975):

"Fana is not a destruction of the individual's essence, but a passing away of his attributes in the attributes of God."

Rumi expresses this idea beautifully in these lines:

"I dissolved in the sea, became a fish.
I dissolved in the cloud, became a bird.
I dissolved in the earth, became a flower.
Whatever I dissolved into, I became that."

This dissolution of the self leads to the state of ecstasy, where the boundaries between lover and beloved, human and divine, dissolve. Rumi often describes this state using the metaphor of the moth and the flame:

"The moth sees light and goes into fire.
You should see fire and go towards light.
Fire is what of heat appears,
While light is the source of fire."

Here, the moth represents the spiritual seeker, drawn irresistibly to the divine flame. The ecstasy of union is so overwhelming that the moth willingly sacrifices itself in the fire. Yet Rumi suggests that true wisdom lies in seeing beyond the apparent "fire" of ecstatic experiences to the "light" of divine reality that is their source.

It's important to note that for Rumi, surrender and ecstasy are not just internal, mystical experiences, but should manifest in our actions and relationships with others. He writes:

> "Be a lamp, or a lifeboat, or a ladder.
> Help someone's soul heal.
> Walk out of your house like a shepherd."

This outward expression of inner transformation is a key aspect of Rumi's teaching. The ecstasy of divine union should lead to greater compassion and service to others.

Rumi also emphasizes that the path of surrender and ecstasy is not always easy. It often involves pain and struggle (Rumi, The Essential Rumi):

> "The wound is the place where the Light enters you."

This perspective transforms even our difficulties and sufferings into opportunities for divine encounter. Every challenge becomes an invitation to deeper surrender, every pain a doorway to ecstasy.

In exploring these themes, Rumi continually pushes us beyond our comfort zones, challenging us to embrace a love that consumes everything:

> "Love is reckless; not reason.
> Reason seeks a profit.
> Love comes on strong, consuming herself, unabashed."

This reckless, consuming love is the essence of Rumi's path of surrender and ecstasy. It's a love that holds nothing back, that gambles everything on the divine encounter.

As we reflect on these teachings, we might ask ourselves: How can we cultivate this spirit of total surrender in our own lives? How might we open ourselves to moments of ecstasy in our everyday experiences? What would it mean to "gamble everything for love" in our spiritual practice?

Rumi's poetry invites us into a way of being that is both deeply challenging and profoundly liberating. It calls us to die to our small, separate sense of self and to be reborn in the vastness of divine love. As he says (Rumi, The Essential Rumi):

> "Your task is not to seek for love,

but merely to seek and find all the barriers within yourself
that you have built against it."
May we have the courage to seek out and dissolve these barriers, opening
ourselves fully to the transformative power of surrender and ecstasy.

The Waterwheel
Stay together, friends.
Don't scatter and sleep.
Our friendship is made
of being awake.
The waterwheel accepts water
and turns and gives it away,
weeping.
That way it stays in the garden,
whereas another roundness rolls
through a dry riverbed looking
for what it thinks it wants.
Stay here, quivering with each moment
like a drop of mercury.

This poem beautifully encapsulates Rumi's teachings on spiritual awakening, surrender, and the transformative power of love. The waterwheel metaphor represents the soul that accepts the flow of divine love (water) and gives it away freely, staying rooted in the spiritual garden. The contrast with the "other roundness" (perhaps representing the ego) that restlessly seeks what it thinks it wants, highlights the peace that comes with surrender. The final image of quivering "like a drop of mercury" evokes the ecstatic state of being fully present and responsive to each moment. This poem aligns perfectly with the chapter's exploration of Rumi's later years and his enduring impact on spiritual thought.

Part II: The Art and Heart of Rumi

Chapter 4: Poetic Alchemy: Rumi's Literary Genius

To understand Rumi's enduring impact, we must delve into the artistry that makes his poetry so powerful. Rumi was not just a mystic with profound insights; he was a master craftsman of language, capable of transmuting the base metal of ordinary experience into the gold of spiritual illumination.

Rumi's poetic style is characterized by several key elements:

1. Vivid Imagery:

Rumi had an extraordinary ability to convey abstract spiritual concepts through concrete, often startling images. Consider these lines (Rumi, The Essential Rumi):

> "The minute I heard my first love story,
> I started looking for you, not knowing
> how blind that was.
> Lovers don't finally meet somewhere.
> They're in each other all along."

Here, the abstract concept of divine love is made tangible through the image of lovers searching for each other, only to realize they've been united all along. This technique allows readers to grasp complex spiritual truths on an intuitive, emotional level.

2. Paradox and Contradiction:

Rumi frequently employs paradox to jolt his readers out of conventional thinking. For example (Rumi, Masnavi):

> "Sell your cleverness and buy bewilderment.
> Cleverness is mere opinion, bewilderment is intuition."

By juxtaposing seemingly contradictory ideas, Rumi invites us to transcend dualistic thinking and glimpse the unity underlying apparent opposites.

3. Ecstatic Rhythm:

Many of Rumi's poems have a rhythmic quality that mirrors the ecstatic state they describe. This is particularly evident in his ghazals, which often build to a crescendo of spiritual intoxication (Rumi, The Essential Rumi):

> "Dance, when you're broken open.
> Dance, if you've torn the bandage off.

Dance in the middle of the fighting.
Dance in your blood.
Dance when you're perfectly free."

The repetition and mounting intensity create a kind of verbal whirling, drawing the reader into the poet's ecstatic state.

4. Everyday Metaphors:

Rumi had a gift for finding the sacred in the mundane. He often uses everyday objects and experiences as metaphors for spiritual truths (Rumi, The Essential Rumi):

"You are not a drop in the ocean.
You are the entire ocean in a drop."

This ability to see the infinite in the finite, the extraordinary in the ordinary, is a hallmark of Rumi's genius.

5. Direct Address:

Many of Rumi's poems are framed as direct addresses - to God, to Shams, to the reader. This creates an intimate, conversational tone that draws the reader into a personal relationship with the divine:

"Come, come, whoever you are.
Wanderer, worshiper, lover of leaving.
It doesn't matter.
Ours is not a caravan of despair.
Come, even if you have broken your vows a thousand times.
Come, yet again, come, come."

This direct appeal bypasses the intellect and speaks straight to the heart, creating a sense of immediacy and urgency.

6. Narrative Poetry:

In addition to his lyric poems, Rumi was a master of narrative poetry, particularly in his magnum opus, the Masnavi. He uses stories - some drawn from Islamic tradition, others from folk tales or his own imagination - to illustrate spiritual principles. These stories often have surprising twists or morals that challenge conventional wisdom:

"A man knocked at a house to beg for a piece of bread. The owner said, 'This is not a bakery.' 'Might you have a bit of gristle then?' 'Do you see a butcher shop here?' 'A little flour?' 'Do you hear a grinding stone?' 'Some water?' 'This is not a well.' Whatever the dervish asked for, the man made some tired joke and refused to give him anything."

Through such stories, Rumi engages our narrative imagination, making complex spiritual teachings accessible and memorable.

7. Mixing of Registers:

Rumi was not afraid to mix the sublime with the earthy, the spiritual with the sensual. His poetry can shift rapidly from lofty mystical insights to bawdy humor or everyday observations. This reflects his holistic vision of spirituality as encompassing all aspects of human experience.

8. Open-ended Symbolism:

Rumi's use of symbolism is rich and multifaceted. Symbols like wine, the tavern, the beloved, or the mirror can take on different meanings in different contexts, allowing for multiple layers of interpretation.

> "I am so small I can barely be seen.
> How can this great love be inside me?
> Look at your eyes. They are small,
> but they see enormous things."

Here, the eyes become a symbol for the paradox of human nature - our apparent insignificance contrasted with our capacity for vast awareness and love.

Rumi's poetic genius lies not just in his mastery of these techniques, but in his ability to use them in service of a profound spiritual vision. His poetry is not mere artistry for its own sake, but a means of transmission - a way of conveying states of consciousness that transcend ordinary language. In Rumi's hands, poetry becomes a kind of spiritual alchemy, transforming the lead of ordinary perception into the gold of mystical insight. He invites us not just to read his words, but to enter into the state of consciousness from which they emerge. As he says (Rumi: The Essential Rumi):

> "Don't be satisfied with stories, how things have gone with others. Unfold your own myth."

In the next chapter, we will explore the personality and character that gave birth to this extraordinary body of work, seeking to understand the man behind the poetry.

The Sunrise Ruby

> In the early morning hour,
> just before dawn, lover and beloved wake
> and take a drink of water.
> She asks, "Do you love me or yourself more?
> Really, tell the absolute truth."
> He says, "There's nothing left of me.
> I'm like a ruby held up to the sunrise.
> Is it still a stone, or a world
> made of redness? It has no resistance
> to sunlight."

This is how Hallaj said, I am God,
and told the truth!
The ruby and the sunrise are one.
Be courageous and discipline yourself.
Completely become hearing and ear,
and wear this sun-ruby as an earring.
Work. Keep digging your well.
Don't think about getting off from work.
Water is there somewhere.
Submit to a daily practice.
Your loyalty to that
is a ring on the door.
Keep knocking, and the joy inside
will eventually open a window
and look out to see who's there.

This poem beautifully illustrates Rumi's poetic genius, incorporating many of the elements discussed in the chapter:

Vivid Imagery: The ruby held up to the sunrise is a powerful visual metaphor for spiritual transformation.

Paradox: The question of whether the ruby is still a stone or has become the redness itself presents a paradoxical concept.

Everyday Metaphors: Water and digging a well are used to represent spiritual seeking and practice.

Direct Address: The poem speaks directly to the reader, offering guidance and encouragement.

Mixing of Registers: It moves from the intimate scene of lovers to profound spiritual concepts.

Open-ended Symbolism: The ruby, sunrise, and water all function as multifaceted spiritual symbols.

The poem encapsulates the alchemical nature of Rumi's poetry, transforming the ordinary (a ruby, a sunrise, digging a well) into profound spiritual teachings about self-dissolution, divine union, and the importance of consistent spiritual practice.

Chapter 5: The Personality of a Saint: Rumi's Character and Qualities

To truly understand Rumi's poetry and teachings, it's crucial to explore the personality from which they emerged. While historical accounts can only provide us with glimpses of Rumi's character, these glimpses, combined with what we can infer from his writings, paint a picture of a remarkable individual whose personal qualities were as extraordinary as his poetic gifts.

1. Humility:

Despite his vast learning and spiritual attainments, Rumi was known for his profound humility. He often emphasized the importance of emptying oneself to become a vessel for divine love (Rumi, The Essential Rumi):

> "You are not a drop in the ocean.
> You are the entire ocean in a drop."

This humility wasn't merely rhetorical; it was reflected in his interactions with people from all walks of life. He was known to bow to children and treat the lowliest members of society with the same respect he accorded to nobles and scholars.

2. Compassion:

Rumi's compassion was legendary. His teachings consistently emphasize the importance of kindness and empathy, not just towards those we love, but towards all beings:

"Be a lamp, or a lifeboat, or a ladder.
Help someone's soul heal.
Walk out of your house like a shepherd."

This compassion extended even to those who opposed or criticized him. There are stories of Rumi responding to hostility with such genuine love that his detractors were transformed into devoted followers.

3. Inclusivity:

In an era marked by religious and cultural divisions, Rumi stood out for his inclusive vision. He welcomed people of all faiths and backgrounds, seeing beyond external differences to the essential unity of all beings:

"Not Christian or Jew or Muslim, not Hindu,
Buddhist, Sufi, or Zen. Not any religion
or cultural system..."

This inclusivity wasn't just theoretical; it was reflected in the diverse following he attracted, which included Muslims, Christians, Jews, and even those considered heretics by the orthodox establishment.

4. Passion:

Rumi was not a dry, ascetic figure, but a man of intense passion. His poetry often speaks of the importance of whole-hearted engagement with life and with the divine (Rumi: The Essential Rumi):

"Let the beauty we love be what we do.
There are hundreds of ways to kneel and kiss the ground."

This passion manifested not just in his spiritual life, but in his relationships, his teaching, and his creative expression. The image of Rumi spontaneously beginning to whirl in ecstatic dance in the marketplace captures this quality of passionate engagement.

5. Playfulness:

Despite the profound nature of his teachings, Rumi maintained a sense of playfulness and humor. His works are peppered with jokes, wordplay, and stories that poke fun at human foibles:

"Knock, And He'll open the door
Vanish, And He'll make you shine like the sun
Fall, And He'll raise you to the heavens
Become nothing, And He'll turn you into everything."

This playfulness served not just to entertain, but to disarm the ego and open listeners to deeper truths.

6. Authenticity:

Rumi consistently emphasized the importance of being true to one's inner nature rather than conforming to external expectations:

"Everyone has been made for some particular work,
and the desire for that work has been put in every heart."

He lived this principle, radically transforming his life after his encounter with Shams despite the scandal it caused among his more conventional followers.

7. Courage:

Rumi displayed remarkable courage in following his spiritual path, even when it led him to break with social conventions. His willingness to risk his reputation and social standing for the sake of spiritual truth is a recurring theme in his life story:

"Run from what's comfortable. Forget safety.
Live where you fear to live. Destroy your reputation.
Be notorious."

8. Generosity:

Accounts of Rumi's life consistently emphasize his generosity, both material and spiritual. He gave freely of his time, his wisdom, and his material resources:

"There are a thousand ways to kneel and kiss the ground;
there are a thousand ways to go home again."

This generosity extended to his creative output; he viewed his poetry not as a personal possession, but as a gift to be shared freely.

9. Presence:

Perhaps the most striking quality attributed to Rumi by his contemporaries was his extraordinary presence. He had the ability to be fully present in each moment, bringing his complete attention to whoever or whatever was before him:

> "This is now. Now is, all there is. Don't wait for Then;
> strike the spark, light the fire."

This quality of presence allowed him to see the divine in every person and situation, transforming ordinary interactions into opportunities for spiritual awakening.

10. Experiential Wisdom:

Rumi emphasized the importance of direct experience over mere intellectual understanding. He often used provocative methods to shake his disciples out of complacency and into a more immediate awareness of spiritual realities.

11. Love:

Central to Rumi's teaching was the transformative power of love. He saw love not just as an emotion, but as the fundamental force of the universe and the key to spiritual awakening. Above all, Rumi was characterized by his capacity for love - not just romantic or personal love, but a all-encompassing, divine love that saw the beloved in all things (Rumi, The Essential Rumi):

> "Your task is not to seek for love,
> but merely to seek and find all the barriers within yourself
> that you have built against it."

This love was not an abstract concept for Rumi, but a lived reality that infused every aspect of his being and his interactions with others.

12. Embracing Paradox:

Rumi was comfortable with paradox and contradiction, seeing them as essential aspects of spiritual truth. He often used seemingly contradictory statements to point towards a reality beyond dualistic thinking:

> "Silence is the language of God, all else is poor translation."

13. Rumi's Daily Life and Practices:

While much of what we know about Rumi's daily life comes from hagiographic accounts that may be embellished, certain patterns emerge:

- Regular Meditation and Prayer: Rumi was devoted to traditional Islamic practices of prayer and meditation, but he infused these with a depth of mystical understanding.

- Sama: The practice of spiritual listening and ecstatic dance became an important part of Rumi's spiritual routine, especially in his later years.

- Teaching and Counseling: Rumi spent much of his time teaching and offering spiritual guidance to a wide range of seekers.

- Poetry and Writing: The composition of poetry became for Rumi a form of spiritual practice and a way of transmitting mystical insights.

14. The Legacy of Rumi's Character:

Rumi's personal qualities were inseparable from his teachings. His humility, compassion, inclusivity, and passion weren't just admirable traits, but living embodiments of his spiritual philosophy. In contemplating these qualities, we begin to see how Rumi's personal character and his spiritual teachings were inextricably intertwined.

In contemplating these qualities, we begin to see how Rumi's personal character and his spiritual teachings were inextricably intertwined. His poetry wasn't just beautiful words on a page, but an expression of a lived reality - a way of being in the world that was as profound as it was inspiring.

As we seek to understand and apply Rumi's teachings in our own lives, it's worth reflecting on how we might cultivate these qualities in ourselves. For Rumi, spiritual growth wasn't about adhering to rigid doctrines or practices, but about embodying these qualities of love, presence, authenticity, and compassion in our daily lives.

In the next chapter, we'll explore how Rumi's unique combination of poetic genius and spiritual insight has influenced not just Islamic mysticism, but world literature and spirituality as a whole.

The Essence of Human

Your hope of good from others is an evil,
Know this for certain; hope only from God.
The least exertion with His aid is much,
The greatest without it is naught.
If you have not seen the devil's snare,
You may have seen the devil's friends.
Do not hand and foot like a beast of burden,

> Come into the state of a man, and escape from the stable.
>> Your eminence and your wealth will not save you;
>> Strip yourself bare of these and enter the arena.
>> Think how this body becomes dust in the grave;
>> The soul which does not go there, whither goes it?

This poem reflects several of Rumi's personal qualities mentioned in the chapter:

Humility: The poem emphasizes reliance on God rather than on oneself or others.

Courage: It encourages facing life's challenges directly, "stripped bare" of worldly attachments.

Authenticity: The call to "come into the state of a man" speaks to being true to one's essential nature.

Spiritual focus: The poem redirects attention from worldly concerns to spiritual matters.

Wisdom: It offers insights into the transient nature of worldly status and the importance of spiritual cultivation.

This poem encapsulates Rumi's approach to spiritual life, emphasizing humility, courage, authenticity, and a focus on the eternal rather than the temporary. It showcases his ability to convey profound spiritual truths through direct, powerful language.

Chapter 6: Rumi's Influence: From Medieval Persia to the Modern World

The reach of Rumi's words extends far beyond the boundaries of time and culture in which they were written. His poetry has not only shaped the landscape of Islamic mysticism but has also profoundly influenced world literature, spirituality, and even popular culture. In this chapter, we'll explore the breadth and depth of Rumi's impact across centuries and continents.

1. Influence on Islamic Mysticism

Within the Islamic world, Rumi's impact was immediate and enduring. The Mevlevi Order, founded by his followers after his death, became one of the most influential Sufi orders, spreading his teachings throughout the Ottoman Empire and beyond. The practice of Sama, the whirling meditation that Rumi originated, became a powerful symbol of Sufi spirituality.

Rumi's Masnavi became known as "the Quran in Persian," studied and revered by Sufis across the Islamic world. His emphasis on divine love as the core of spirituality influenced generations of mystics, including the great Andalusian Sufi Ibn Arabi and the Persian poet Hafiz.

2. Impact on Persian Literature

Rumi's innovations in Persian poetry were groundbreaking. He expanded the possibilities of the ghazal form, infusing it with mystical meaning, and his use of everyday language and imagery to convey profound spiritual truths set a new standard for Persian literature. Poets like Saadi, Hafiz, and Jami all show the influence of Rumi's style and themes.

3. Transmission to the West

Rumi's introduction to the Western world came gradually. In the 19th century, orientalists like Sir William Jones and R.A. Nicholson began translating his works into European languages. However, it was in the 20th century that Rumi truly captured the Western imagination.

The translations and interpretations of Coleman Barks in the 1970s and beyond played a crucial role in popularizing Rumi in the English-speaking world. Barks' free adaptations of Rumi's poetry, while controversial among some scholars, struck a chord with modern readers and helped make Rumi the best-selling poet in the United States.

4. Influence on Western Literature and Thought

Rumi's poetry has influenced Western writers and thinkers from Goethe to Emerson. His emphasis on the unity underlying all religions resonated with the Transcendentalist movement in 19th century America. In the 20th century, writers like Robert Bly and John Moyne drew inspiration from Rumi in their own poetic and spiritual explorations.

Rumi's ideas have also found their way into Western philosophy and psychology. His concept of the human being as a microcosm of the divine, and his emphasis on love as a transformative force, have parallels in the work of Carl Jung and other depth psychologists.

5. Impact on Contemporary Spirituality

In the late 20th and early 21st centuries, Rumi has become a central figure in the Western spiritual landscape. His non-dogmatic approach to spirituality, emphasis on direct experience, and celebration of love and ecstasy have made him a touchstone for many seeking alternatives to traditional religious paths.

Rumi's poetry is often quoted in yoga classes, meditation retreats, and interfaith gatherings. His words have become a kind of universal spiritual language, bridging differences between various faiths and philosophies (Rumi, The Essential Rumi):

> "Out beyond ideas of wrongdoing and right doing,
> there is a field. I'll meet you there."

6. Influence on Popular Culture

Rumi's reach extends even into popular culture. His poetry has been set to music by numerous artists, from traditional Persian musicians to Western pop stars. His words appear on greeting cards, inspirational posters, and social media posts. While this popularization has sometimes led to oversimplification of his message, it has also introduced his wisdom to audiences who might never have encountered it otherwise.

7. Controversies and Criticisms

The widespread adoption of Rumi in the West has not been without controversy. Some scholars argue that many popular translations, particularly those of Coleman Barks, take too many liberties with the original text, removing specifically Islamic references and creating a "New Age Rumi" that bears little resemblance to the 13th-century Sufi master.

There are also concerns about cultural appropriation, with critics arguing that the Western embrace of Rumi often ignores or minimizes his Muslim identity and the Islamic context of his work.

8. Rumi's Relevance Today

Despite these controversies, Rumi's popularity shows no signs of waning. In a world often divided by religious and cultural differences, his message of universal love and spiritual unity continues to resonate. His poetry speaks to the human longing for meaning, connection, and transcendence in a way that crosses cultural boundaries (Rumi, The Essential Rumi):

"What you seek is seeking you."

In an age of environmental crisis, his vision of the interconnectedness of all beings offers a spiritual foundation for ecological awareness:

"The beauty of the heart

is the lasting beauty:

its lips give to drink

of the water of life."

In a time of rapid technological change and information overload, his emphasis on direct experience and the wisdom of the heart provides a much-needed counterbalance (Rumi, Masnavi):

"Sell your cleverness and buy bewilderment.

Cleverness is mere opinion, bewilderment is intuition."

As we face the challenges of the 21st century, Rumi's words continue to offer guidance, inspiration, and solace. His enduring popularity is a testament to the universal nature of his message and the timeless power of his poetry.

In the chapters that follow, we will delve deeper into the major themes of Rumi's work, exploring how his teachings can be applied to our lives today. But as we do so, let us remember that Rumi's true legacy lies not in words on a page, but in the transformation those words can inspire in our hearts and in our world (Rumi: The Essential Rumi).

"Let the beauty we love be what we do.
There are hundreds of ways to kneel and kiss the ground."

At the heart of Rumi's poetry lies a profound mystical vision—a direct, experiential knowledge of the divine that transcends intellectual understanding. This mystical dimension is not an abstract philosophy, but a lived reality that infuses every aspect of Rumi's work with a sense of wonder, ecstasy, and transformative power.

As scholar William C. Chittick notes in "The Sufi Path of Love: The Spiritual Teachings of Rumi" (1983), "For Rumi, mysticism is not about extraordinary experiences or supernatural powers, but about recognizing the extraordinary within the ordinary, the divine presence that permeates all of existence."

Rumi's mysticism is grounded in the Sufi concept of "wahdat al-wujud" or the unity of existence. This perspective sees all of creation as a manifestation of divine reality. As Rumi expresses it:
"I looked for God among the Christians and on the Cross and therein I found Him not.
I went into the ancient temples of idolatry; no trace of Him was there.
I entered the mountain cave of Hira and then went as far as Qandhar but God I found not.
With set purpose I fared to the summit of Mount Caucasus and found there only 'anqa's habitation.
Then I directed my search to the Kaaba, the resort of old and young; God was not there even.
Turning to philosophy I inquired about him from ibn Sina but found Him not within his range.
I fared then to the scene of the Prophet's experience of a great divine manifestation only a
"two bow-lengths' distance from him" but God was not there even in that

exalted court.

Finally, I looked into my own heart and there I saw Him; He was nowhere else."

This powerful passage illustrates the core of Rumi's mystical vision—the recognition that the divine is not to be found in external forms or places, but in the depths of one's own being.

Rumi's mysticism is characterized by a passionate, personal relationship with the divine. He often speaks of God as the Beloved, using the language of human love to express the intensity of spiritual longing and union (Rumi, The Essential Rumi):

"The minute I heard my first love story,
I started looking for you, not knowing
how blind that was.
Lovers don't finally meet somewhere.
They're in each other all along."

This intimate, loving relationship with the divine is at the core of Rumi's mystical practice. It transforms every moment into an opportunity for communion, every experience into a revelation of divine presence.

Another key aspect of Rumi's mysticism is the concept of "fana" or annihilation in God. This is not a destruction of the self, but a transcendence of the limited ego-self and a realization of one's true nature as inseparable from the divine. Rumi expresses this state in various ways:

"I dissolved in the sea, became a fish.
I dissolved in the cloud, became a bird.
I dissolved in the earth, became a flower.
Whatever I dissolved into, I became that."

This dissolution of the separate self leads to the state of "baqa" or subsistence in God, where one lives from the center of divine consciousness. It's a state of perpetual wonder and gratitude, where every atom of creation is recognized as a mirror of divine beauty.

Rumi's mysticism is not about escaping the world, but about seeing it with new eyes. He invites us to recognize the sacred in the ordinary, to see every experience as a theophany—a manifestation of divine presence. As he writes:

"Today, like every other day, we wake up empty
and frightened. Don't open the door to the study

and begin reading. Take down a musical instrument.
Let the beauty we love be what we do.
There are hundreds of ways to kneel and kiss the ground."
This perspective transforms daily life into a continuous act of worship, where every action becomes a way of "kneeling and kissing the ground."

Central to Rumi's mystical vision is the practice of remembrance or "dhikr." This is not merely a mental recollection, but a whole-being awareness of divine presence. Rumi often expresses this through the metaphor of music:
"We have fallen into the place
where everything is music."
This music is not just an auditory experience, but a resonance with the divine harmony that underlies all of existence.

Rumi's mysticism also emphasizes the importance of direct experience over secondhand knowledge. He frequently critiques those who rely solely on book learning or religious dogma:
"The Sufi opens his hands to the universe
and gives away each instant, free.
Unlike someone who begs on the street for money to survive,
a dervish begs to give you his life."
This openness to experience, this willingness to "give away each instant," is at the heart of Rumi's mystical path.

Yet Rumi is also keenly aware of the limitations of language in conveying mystical truth. He often points to a reality beyond words (Rumi, The Essential Rumi):
"Silence is the language of God,
all else is poor translation."
This silence is not an absence of sound, but a profound presence that transcends conceptual thought.

Rumi's mysticism is not a path of withdrawal from the world, but of engaged presence. It calls us to recognize the divine in every face we encounter:
"The beauty you see in me is a reflection of you."
This perspective fosters a radical inclusivity and compassion, seeing every being as a unique expression of divine beauty.

As we contemplate Rumi's mystical vision, we're invited to open ourselves to a deeper dimension of reality. We're challenged to move beyond our habitual patterns of perception to recognize the extraordinary within the ordinary. We're encouraged to cultivate a loving, personal relationship with the divine that infuses every aspect of our lives.

May we carry this mystical awareness into our daily lives, recognizing each moment as an opportunity for divine encounter. For as Rumi reminds us (Rumi, The Essential Rumi):

"You are not a drop in the ocean.
You are the entire ocean in a drop."

In this simple, profound statement, Rumi captures the essence of his mystical vision—a recognition of our true nature as inseparable from the divine whole, an invitation to awaken to the infinite within the finite.

The Pickaxe

The Mathnawi is a pickaxe to break open
the frozen soil, the closed heart.
Someone who does not work with this pickaxe
is a bird without wings, a fly without feet.
Don't turn your face away. Keep looking
at the bandaged place. That's where
the light enters you.
And don't believe for a moment
that you're healing yourself.

This poem reflects several key aspects of Rumi's mysticism and influence:

1. The transformative power of spiritual teachings (the Mathnawi as a "pickaxe")

2. The importance of inner work and self-reflection

3. The idea that our wounds can be sources of spiritual growth ("where the light enters you")

4. Humility in acknowledging a higher power in the process of spiritual healing

This poem encapsulates Rumi's approach to spirituality, emphasizing the need for active engagement with spiritual teachings and the transformative potential of facing our inner struggles.

Part III: Divine Flirtations - Themes in Rumi's Wisdom

Chapter 7: The Beloved: Divine and Human Love

At the heart of Rumi's poetry lies the concept of love - not merely human love, but a divine, all-encompassing love that permeates the universe. For Rumi, love is not just an emotion or a sentiment, but the very essence of existence, the force that moves the cosmos and drives all of creation. This chapter will explore Rumi's unique perspective on love and its transformative power.

1. The Beloved as Divine

In Rumi's poetry, the figure of the Beloved is multifaceted. On one level, it represents the Divine itself - God, or what Rumi often calls "the Friend." This divine Beloved is both transcendent and immanent, beyond all form yet present in every atom of creation:

> "I am the dust in the sunlight, I am the ball of the sun
> I am the mist of morning, the breath of evening
> I am the spark in the stone, the gleam of gold in the metal
> The rose and the nightingale drunk with its fragrance
> I am the chain of being, the circle of the spheres
> The scale of creation, the rise and the fall
> I am what is and is not, I am, I am"

For Rumi, the entire universe is an expression of divine love, and every form of love - whether between humans, or between humans and nature - is ultimately a reflection of this divine love.

2. The Interplay of Human and Divine Love

While Rumi often speaks of the Divine Beloved, he doesn't dismiss human love. Instead, he sees human love as a bridge to divine love. His own transformative relationship with Shams of Tabriz is a prime example of how human love can open the door to mystical experience (Rumi, The Essential Rumi):

"The minute I heard my first love story,
I started looking for you, not knowing
how blind that was.
Lovers don't finally meet somewhere.
They're in each other all along."

In Rumi's view, falling in love with another person can be a first step towards falling in love with the Divine. The intensity and selflessness of human love can give us a taste of the all-consuming love that mystics feel for God.

3. Love as Transformative Power

For Rumi, love is not just a feeling, but a transformative power that can reshape our very being (Rumi, The Essential Rumi):

"Your task is not to seek for love,
but merely to seek and find all the barriers within yourself
that you have built against it."

Love, in this sense, is a purifying fire that burns away the ego and all that separates us from the Divine. It's a force that can turn us inside out, breaking down our preconceptions and opening us to new dimensions of reality:

"Love comes with a knife, not some shy question,
and not with fears for its reputation!"

4. The Pain of Separation

A recurring theme in Rumi's poetry is the pain of separation from the Beloved. This sense of separation - what Sufis call firaq - is seen as a necessary stage in the spiritual journey. It creates the longing (shauq) that drives the seeker towards reunion (Rumi, The Essential Rumi):

"The wound is the place where the Light enters you."

Rumi often uses the image of the reed flute, separated from its reed bed, to symbolize this state of separation:

"Listen to the story told by the reed,
of being separated.

Since I was cut from the reedbed,
I have made this crying sound."

73

5. The Joy of Union

While Rumi speaks often of the pain of separation, his poetry also celebrates the ecstatic joy of union with the Beloved. This state of union, or fana, is the goal of the Sufi path:

"I have been tricked by flying too close
to what I thought I loved.
Now the candle flame is out, the wine spilled,
and the lovers have withdrawn somewhere beyond my reach.
I have been fooled by love too many times to count.
I have been emptied
and refilled
like a wineglass."

In this state of union, the boundaries between lover and beloved, between self and other, dissolve. The seeker recognizes that what they sought was within them all along:

"I searched for God among the Christians and on the Cross and therein I found Him not.
I went into the ancient temples of idolatry; no trace of Him was there.
I entered the mountain cave of Hira and then went as far as Qandhar but God I found not.
With set purpose I fared to the summit of Mount Caucasus and found there only 'anqa's habitation.
Then I directed my search to the Kaaba, the resort of old and young; God was not there even.
Turning to philosophy I inquired about him from ibn Sina but found Him not within his range.
I fared then to the scene of the Prophet's experience of a great divine manifestation only a "two bow-lengths' distance from him" but God was not there even in that exalted court.
Finally, I looked into my own heart and there I saw Him; He was nowhere else."

6. Love as the Core of Spirituality

Ultimately, for Rumi, love is not just an aspect of spirituality - it is its very essence. All spiritual practices, all religious doctrines, are merely vehicles for cultivating this fundamental reality of love:

"All religions, all this singing, one song.
The differences are just illusion and vanity.
The sun's light looks a little different
on this wall than it does on that wall,
and a lot different on this other one,
but it's still one light."

In Rumi's vision, love is the force that created the universe, the energy that sustains it, and the magnet that draws all beings back to their source. To awaken to love is to awaken to the true nature of reality:

"Love is the whole thing.
We are only pieces."

As we reflect on Rumi's teachings on love, we might ask ourselves: How can we cultivate this all-encompassing love in our own lives? How might our perspective shift if we saw all forms of love as reflections of the divine? And how might our world change if we, like Rumi, placed love at the center of our spiritual and everyday lives?

In the next chapter, we will explore another central theme in Rumi's work: the path of longing and spiritual seeking.

Love Dogs

One night a man was crying,
Allah! Allah!
His lips grew sweet with the praising,
until a cynic said,
"So! I have heard you
calling out, but have you ever
gotten any response?"
The man had no answer to that.
He quit praying and fell into a confused sleep.
He dreamed he saw Khidr, the guide of souls,
in a thick, green foliage.
"Why did you stop praising?"
"Because I've never heard anything back."
"This longing
you express is the return message."
The grief you cry out from
draws you toward union.
Your pure sadness
that wants help
is the secret cup.
Listen to the moan of a dog for its master.
That whining is the connection.
There are love dogs
no one knows the names of.
Give your life
to be one of them.

This poem beautifully encapsulates several key ideas from the chapter:

1. The interplay between human and divine love
2. The pain of separation as a driving force towards union
3. The transformative power of love
4. Love as the core of spirituality
5. The idea that longing itself is a form of connection to the divine

The poem illustrates Rumi's perspective that even when we feel unheard or separated from the divine, our very longing is a form of connection. It encourages persistence in love and devotion, even in the face of apparent silence, reflecting Rumi's teachings on the spiritual journey of love.

Chapter 8: The Path of Longing: Spiritual Seeking

In Rumi's poetry, the journey towards the Divine is often characterized by an intense longing, a yearning that propels the seeker forward on their spiritual path. This longing, or 'shauq' in Sufi terminology, is not seen as a negative state to be overcome, but as a vital force in spiritual growth. Let's explore this theme in depth.

1. The Nature of Spiritual Longing

For Rumi, spiritual longing is not a mere desire for something external, but a deep, innate yearning of the soul to return to its source. He often describes this longing using powerful metaphors (Rumi, The Essential Rumi):

"There is a candle in your heart, ready to be kindled.

There is a void in your soul, ready to be filled.

You feel it, don't you?"

This longing is seen as evidence of our divine origin and destiny. It's the pull of the ocean felt by a drop of water, the attraction of the flame experienced by the moth (Rumi, The Essential Rumi):

"The wound is the place where the Light enters you."

Closely linked to love in Rumi's poetry is the theme of spiritual longing. This longing, or 'ishq' in Sufi terminology, is seen as evidence of our divine origin and destiny. It's the force that propels the seeker on their journey [10]:

"There is a candle in your heart, ready to be kindled.

There is a void in your soul, ready to be filled.

You feel it, don't you?"

2. Longing as a Catalyst for Transformation

In Rumi's view, this spiritual longing serves as a catalyst for inner transformation. It's the force that drives us to look beyond the surface of things, to seek deeper meaning and connection (Rumi: The Essential Rumi):

"Don't be satisfied with stories, how things have gone with others. Unfold your own myth."

The discomfort of longing pushes us out of complacency and sets us on the path of seeking:

"Run from what's comfortable. Forget safety.

Live where you fear to live. Destroy your reputation.
Be notorious."

3. The Paradox of Seeking

One of the paradoxes that Rumi often explores is that what we seek is already within us. The journey of seeking, then, is not about finding something external, but about uncovering what's already there:

"Why are you so enchanted by this world, when a mine of gold lies within you?"

This doesn't mean that seeking is unnecessary, but rather that the process of seeking itself is transformative, gradually unveiling our true nature (Rumi, The Essential Rumi):

"What you seek is seeking you."

4. The Role of Patience and Perseverance

While Rumi celebrates the intensity of longing, he also emphasizes the importance of patience and perseverance on the spiritual path. The journey is not always easy or straightforward:

"Patience is not sitting and waiting, it is foreseeing. It is looking at the thorn and seeing the rose, looking at the night and seeing the day. Lovers are patient and know that the moon needs time to become full."

He encourages seekers to persist even when the path seems difficult or unclear:

"Keep walking, though there's no place to get to.

Don't try to see through the distances.

That's not for human beings. Move within,

but don't move the way fear makes you move."

5. The Interplay of Absence and Presence

In Rumi's poetry, the experience of longing is often intertwined with a sense of the Beloved's absence. Yet paradoxically, this very sense of absence can be a form of presence:

"Absence is a strange land. Its borders are everywhere,

But its center is nowhere.

Sometimes in the heart of absence, in its very marrow,

I feel your presence."

This interplay of absence and presence creates a dynamic tension that fuels the spiritual journey (Rumi, The Essential Rumi):

"I have lived on the lip of insanity, wanting to know reasons,

knocking on a door. It opens.

I've been knocking from the inside."

6. Longing as a Form of Praise

For Rumi, the longing itself becomes a form of worship, a way of praising the Divine:

"This longing you express is the return message.

The grief you cry out from

draws you toward union.

Your pure sadness

that wants help

is the secret cup."

In this view, even our feelings of separation and yearning are evidence of our connection to the Divine:

"This is love: to fly toward a secret sky,

to cause a hundred veils to fall each moment.

First to let go of life.

Finally, to take a step without feet."

7. The Ultimate Goal: Annihilation in the Beloved

In Sufi thought, the ultimate aim of this longing and seeking is fana, or annihilation in the Divine. Rumi describes this state in various ways:

"I dissolved in the sea, became a fish.

I dissolved in the cloud, became a bird.

I dissolved in the earth, became a flower.

Whatever I dissolved into, I became that."

This state of union is not an end to longing, but its fulfillment and transformation:

"When I am with you, we stay up all night.

When you're not here, I can't go to sleep.

Praise God for those two insomnias!

And the difference between them."

As we reflect on Rumi's teachings about spiritual longing and seeking, we might ask ourselves: What do we truly long for in the depths of our being? How can we cultivate this longing as a positive force in our lives? And how might our perspective on life's challenges shift if we view them as part of this greater journey of seeking and transformation?

In the next chapter, we'll explore another central theme in Rumi's work: the experience of ecstatic union with the Divine.

The Pull of Love

The minute I heard my first love story,
I started looking for you, not knowing
how blind that was.
Lovers don't finally meet somewhere.
They're in each other all along.
We are the mirror as well as the face in it.
We are tasting the taste this minute
of eternity. We are pain
and what cures pain, both.
We are the sweet cold water
and the jar that pours.
I want to hold you close like a lute,
so we can cry out with loving.
You would rather throw stones at a mirror?
I am your mirror, and here are the stones.
Why are you so enchanted by this world
when a mine of gold lies within you?
Fall in love in such a way
that it frees you from any connecting.
Love is the soul's light, the taste of morning,
no me, no we, no claim of being.
These pains you feel are messengers. Listen to them.
Turn them to sweetness. The night is almost over.
The mystery of longing and seeking
knows not what it seeks.

This poem beautifully encapsulates many of the themes discussed in the text about Rumi's perspective on spiritual longing and seeking:

It starts with the idea of seeking something external, not realizing that what we seek is already within us: "I started looking for you, not knowing how blind that was."

It touches on the paradox of seeking, as mentioned in the text: "Lovers don't finally meet somewhere. They're in each other all along."

The poem explores the interplay of absence and presence, pain and healing: "We are pain and what cures pain, both."

It alludes to the transformation that longing can bring about: "These pains you feel are messengers. Listen to them. Turn them to sweetness."

The poem also touches on the theme of spiritual wealth within oneself: "Why are you so enchanted by this world when a mine of gold lies within you?"

Finally, it speaks to the mystery and ineffability of spiritual longing: "The mystery of longing and seeking knows not what it seeks."

This poem, like many of Rumi's works, uses vivid imagery and paradoxical statements to convey the complex nature of spiritual seeking and the relationship between the seeker and the Divine. It reflects many of the ideas discussed in the text about how Rumi viewed spiritual longing as a transformative force in one's life.

Chapter 9: Ecstatic Union: Dissolving into the Divine

One of the most powerful and captivating themes in Rumi's poetry is that of ecstatic union with the Divine. This state, known in Sufi terminology as fana (annihilation) or baqa (subsistence in God), represents the pinnacle of the spiritual journey. Let's delve into Rumi's vivid descriptions and teachings about this transformative experience.

1. The Nature of Ecstatic Union

For Rumi, ecstatic union is not merely a mystical concept, but a lived experience of dissolving into the Divine presence. He describes it as a state where the boundaries between self and other, between human and divine, dissolve:

> "I am not this hair, I am not this skin,
> I am the soul that lives within."

This union is often portrayed as a kind of intoxication, a spiritual drunkenness that transcends ordinary consciousness (Rumi, The Essential Rumi):

> "In your light I learn how to love.
> In your beauty, how to make poems.
> You dance inside my chest where no one sees you,
> but sometimes I do, and that sight becomes this art."

2. The Paradox of Selfhood

Central to Rumi's understanding of ecstatic union is the paradox of selfhood. To achieve union with the Divine, one must paradoxically lose oneself:

"You've seen my descent. Now watch my rising.

'You' is no more. 'I' is no more.

We are one in ecstatic bliss."

This loss of self is not seen as a negation, but as an expansion into a greater reality:

"Why should I seek? I am the same as He.

His essence speaks through me.

I have been looking for myself!"

3. The Imagery of Union

Rumi uses a rich variety of metaphors and images to convey the experience of ecstatic union. Some of the most common include:

- The moth and the flame: "I am the moth, You are the flame.

I am scattered like the dust, You are the wind."

- The drop and the ocean: "You are not a drop in the ocean.

You are the entire ocean in a drop."

- The reed flute: "We are as the flute, and the music in us is from thee;

we are as the mountain and the echo in us is from thee."

4. The Role of Love in Union

For Rumi, love is the force that makes ecstatic union possible. It's through love that the seeker is drawn out of themselves and into the Divine:

"This is love: to fly toward a secret sky,

to cause a hundred veils to fall each moment.

First to let go of life.

Finally, to take a step without feet."

Love, in this context, is not merely an emotion but a transformative power that reshapes the very core of one's being (Rumi, The Essential Rumi):

"Love is the bridge between you and everything."

5. The Dance of Union

One of the most famous expressions of ecstatic union in Rumi's tradition is the practice of Sama, or whirling. This sacred dance, which Rumi is said to have originated, is a physical enactment of the soul's journey towards union with the Divine (Rumi, The Essential Rumi):

"We came whirling out of nothingness,
scattering stars like dust...
The stars made a circle,
and in the middle, we dance."

The circular motion of the dance symbolizes the seeker's journey around the heart, with one hand reaching to heaven and the other to earth, bridging the divine and human realms.

6. The Aftermath of Union

Rumi doesn't shy away from describing the aftermath of ecstatic experiences. He acknowledges that these moments of union are often fleeting, leaving the seeker with a bittersweet longing:

"I have been burned by the sun of union,
struck by the lightning bolt of separation.
In this moment, I am nothing but ashes,
scattered by the wind of longing."

Yet even this separation becomes a form of connection, fueling the seeker's journey (Rumi, The Essential Rumi):

"The wound is the place where the Light enters you."

7. Union as the Goal and the Path

For Rumi, ecstatic union is both the ultimate goal of the spiritual journey and a recurring experience along the way. Each taste of union deepens the seeker's commitment to the path (Rumi, The Essential Rumi):

"There is a candle in your heart, ready to be kindled.
There is a void in your soul, ready to be filled.
You feel it, don't you?"

This reciprocal relationship between seeking and finding, between longing and union, creates a dynamic spiritual life that is always in motion, always unfolding.

8. The Universality of Union

While Rumi's language is often steeped in Islamic and Sufi terminology, his descriptions of ecstatic union have a universal quality that transcends any specific religious framework:

> "Not Christian or Jew or Muslim, not Hindu,
> Buddhist, Sufi, or Zen. Not any religion
> or cultural system. I am not from the East
> or the West, not out of the ocean or up
> from the ground, not natural or ethereal, not
> composed of elements at all. I do not exist,
> am not an entity in this world or the next,
> did not descend from Adam and Eve or any
> origin story. My place is placeless, a trace
> of the traceless. Neither body or soul.
> I belong to the beloved, have seen the two
> worlds as one and that one call to and know,
> first, last, outer, inner, only that
> breath breathing human being."

This universality has contributed to Rumi's enduring appeal across cultures and traditions.

As we contemplate Rumi's teachings on ecstatic union, we might ask ourselves: Have we experienced moments of transcendence or unity in our own lives? How might we cultivate a greater openness to such experiences? And how can we bring the insights gained from moments of "union" into our everyday lives?

One of the most remarkable aspects of Rumi's poetry is its universal appeal. Despite being rooted in Islamic mysticism and written in 13th century Persia, Rumi's words continue to resonate with people across cultures, religions, and time periods. This universality is not incidental, but a core aspect of Rumi's vision of reality and his understanding of love.

As scholar Franklin D. Lewis notes in his comprehensive biography "Rumi - Past and Present, East and West" (2000), "Rumi's poetry speaks to the universal human experience of love, longing, and the search for meaning. His ability to express profound spiritual truths in accessible, often sensual language has given his work an enduring, cross-cultural appeal."

At the heart of Rumi's universal vision is his concept of divine love. For Rumi, love is not just a human emotion, but the very essence of existence, the force that creates and sustains the universe. He writes:

"Love is the water of life. And a lover is a soul of fire!
The universe turns differently when fire loves water."
This cosmic vision of love transcends religious and cultural boundaries. It speaks to a fundamental human intuition that love is not just a personal feeling, but a universal force that connects us all.

Rumi's universality is also reflected in his inclusive approach to religion. While deeply rooted in Islamic tradition, Rumi frequently emphasizes the unity underlying all spiritual paths (Rumi, Divan-e Shams-e Tabrizi):

"The lamps are different,
But the Light is the same."

This perspective allows people of all faiths (and none) to find resonance in Rumi's words. It suggests that the differences between religions are surface-level, while at their core, all authentic spiritual paths lead to the same divine reality.

Perhaps Rumi's most famous expression of this universal spirituality is found in these lines:

"Not Christian or Jew or Muslim, not Hindu,
Buddhist, Sufi, or Zen. Not any religion
or cultural system. I am not from the East
or the West, not out of the ocean or up
from the ground, not natural or ethereal, not
composed of elements at all. I do not exist,
am not an entity in this world or the next,
did not descend from Adam and Eve or any
origin story. My place is placeless, a trace
of the traceless. Neither body or soul.
I belong to the beloved, have seen the two
worlds as one and that one call to and know,
first, last, outer, inner, only that
breath breathing human being."

This powerful statement transcends all categories of identity—religious, cultural, even human—to point to a state of being that is universal and all-encompassing.

Rumi's universality is also evident in his use of everyday metaphors to convey spiritual truths. He draws from nature, from human relationships, from common experiences to illuminate the divine. This makes his poetry accessible to people from all walks of life. For example (Rumi, The Essential Rumi):

"You were born with potential.
You were born with goodness and trust.
You were born with ideals and dreams.

You were born with greatness.
You were born with wings.
You are not meant for crawling, so don't.
You have wings.
Learn to use them and fly."

These words speak to the universal human experience of aspiration and growth. They encourage us to recognize our innate potential, regardless of our background or beliefs.

Rumi's universal vision extends to his understanding of human nature. He sees the divine reflected in every human being:

"The beauty you see in me is a reflection of you."

This perspective invites us to recognize the sacred in ourselves and in every person we encounter, fostering a spirit of unity and compassion.

Even in his treatment of suffering, Rumi offers a universal perspective (Rumi, The Essential Rumi):

"The wound is the place where the Light enters you."

This profound insight speaks to the universal human experience of pain and transformation. It suggests that our very vulnerability can become a source of illumination and growth.

Rumi's universality is not about erasing differences or promoting a bland uniformity. Rather, it's about recognizing a deeper unity that embraces and celebrates diversity. As he says:

"All religions, all this singing, one song.
The differences are just illusion and vanity.
The sun's light looks a little different
on this wall than it does on that wall,
and a lot different on this other one,
but it's still one light."

This metaphor beautifully captures Rumi's vision of unity in diversity. Just as the same sunlight takes on different qualities as it falls on different surfaces, the one divine reality expresses itself in myriad forms throughout creation.

As we contemplate Rumi's universal vision, we're invited to expand our own understanding of spirituality and human connection. We're challenged to look beyond surface differences to recognize the common heart of humanity. We're encouraged to see every encounter, every experience as an opportunity for divine communion.

In a world often divided by religious and cultural differences, Rumi's universal message is perhaps more relevant than ever. It offers a vision of spirituality that is both deeply rooted and radically inclusive, that honors tradition while transcending its boundaries.

May we carry this universal vision into our own lives, recognizing the divine in every face we encounter, seeing every moment as an opportunity for love. For as Rumi reminds us (Rumi, The Essential Rumi):

"We are all just walking each other home."

In this simple, profound statement, Rumi captures the essence of his universal vision—a recognition of our shared journey, our common destination, and the love that binds us all.

In the next chapter, we'll explore another key theme in Rumi's work: the dance of opposites and the embrace of paradox.

Only Breath

Not Christian or Jew or Muslim, not Hindu
Buddhist, sufi, or zen. Not any religion
or cultural system. I am not from the East
or the West, not out of the ocean or up
from the ground, not natural or ethereal, not
composed of elements at all. I do not exist,
am not an entity in this world or the next,
did not descend from Adam and Eve or any
origin story. My place is placeless, a trace
of the traceless. Neither body or soul.
I belong to the beloved, have seen the two
worlds as one and that one call to and know,
first, last, outer, inner, only that
breath breathing human being.

Transcendence of religious and cultural boundaries: The poem begins by explicitly rejecting identification with any specific religion or cultural system, reflecting Rumi's universal vision of spirituality.

Unity beyond duality: The lines "I am not from the East or the West" and "Neither body or soul" speak to Rumi's concept of moving beyond dualistic thinking to a state of unity.

Ecstatic union: The phrase "I belong to the beloved" suggests the intimate connection with the Divine that Rumi often describes.

Non-existence or fana: When Rumi says "I do not exist," he's touching on the Sufi concept of fana or annihilation of the self in the Divine, which is a key aspect of ecstatic union.

Universality of human experience: The final line, "only that breath breathing human being," brings the poem back to the shared essence of all humanity, regardless of religious or cultural differences.

Paradox: The poem is full of paradoxical statements like "My place is placeless," which is characteristic of Rumi's attempts to express ineffable spiritual truths.

This poem beautifully illustrates Rumi's ability to express profound spiritual concepts in a way that transcends specific religious traditions, making his work universally accessible and relevant. It captures the essence of ecstatic union and the dissolution of the self into a greater, all-encompassing reality that Rumi often describes in his poetry.

Chapter 10: The Dance of Opposites: Embracing Paradox

One of the most striking aspects of Rumi's poetry and teachings is his ability to hold and even celebrate apparent contradictions. For Rumi, the spiritual path is not about resolving paradoxes or choosing one side of a duality, but about embracing the dynamic interplay of opposites. This chapter will explore this theme in depth.

1. The Unity of Opposites

At the heart of Rumi's worldview is the idea that apparent opposites are, in reality, different aspects of a greater unity. He often expresses this through vivid imagery:

> "The moment I heard my first love story,
> I started looking for you, not knowing
> how blind that was.
> Lovers don't finally meet somewhere.
> They're in each other all along."

Here, the apparent opposition between seeker and sought, lover and beloved, dissolves into a deeper unity.

2. Beyond Good and Evil

Rumi challenges conventional notions of morality, suggesting that what we perceive as good and evil are part of a greater whole (Rumi, The Essential Rumi):

> "Out beyond ideas of wrongdoing and rightdoing,
> there is a field. I'll meet you there."

This doesn't mean that Rumi advocates moral relativism, but rather that he invites us to see beyond surface-level judgments to the underlying unity of existence.

3. Light and Dark

The interplay of light and darkness is a recurring theme in Rumi's work. Rather than seeing darkness as something to be eliminated, he often portrays it as a necessary complement to light:

> "What hurts you, blesses you.
> Darkness is your candle."

This perspective encourages us to find value and meaning even in difficult or challenging experiences.

4. Joy and Sorrow

Rumi often speaks of joy and sorrow as intimate companions, each giving depth and meaning to the other (Rumi, The Essential Rumi):

"The wound is the place where the Light enters you."

By embracing both joy and sorrow, rather than clinging to one and rejecting the other, we open ourselves to a fuller experience of life.

5. Presence and Absence

The tension between presence and absence, particularly in relation to the Divine, is a central theme in Rumi's work:

> "I have lived on the lip
> of insanity, wanting to know reasons,
> knocking on a door. It opens.
> I've been knocking from the inside."

Here, the apparent absence of the Divine is revealed to be a form of presence, with the seeker and the sought revealed as one.

6. Form and Formlessness

Rumi often plays with the relationship between form and formlessness, particularly in describing the nature of the Divine:

> "I am not this hair, I am not this skin,
> I am the soul that lives within."

This perspective invites us to look beyond surface appearances to the deeper reality that underlies all forms.

7. The Paradox of the Spiritual Journey

Rumi frequently points out the paradoxical nature of the spiritual journey itself (Rumi, The Essential Rumi):

"Your task is not to seek for love,

but merely to seek and find all the barriers within yourself

that you have built against it."

Here, the path to union is not about finding something external, but about removing internal obstacles.

8. The Role of Contradiction in Spiritual Growth

For Rumi, contradictions and paradoxes are not problems to be solved, but opportunities for growth and transformation (Rumi, Masnavi):

"Sell your cleverness and buy bewilderment.

Cleverness is mere opinion, bewilderment is intuition."

By embracing paradox, we move beyond the limitations of rational thought and open ourselves to deeper wisdom.

9. The Dance of Opposites

Rumi often portrays the interplay of opposites as a kind of cosmic dance:

"We are the mirror as well as the face in it.

We are tasting the taste this minute

of eternity. We are pain

and what cures pain, both. We are

the sweet cold water and the jar that pours."

This dance is not about resolving contradictions, but about participating fully in the dynamic flow of life.

10. Transcending Duality

Ultimately, Rumi invites us to transcend duality altogether, to move beyond the realm of opposites into a state of unity:

"Not Christian or Jew or Muslim, not Hindu,

Buddhist, sufi, or zen. Not any religion

or cultural system. I am not from the East

or the West, not out of the ocean or up

from the ground, not natural or ethereal, not

composed of elements at all. I do not exist,

am not an entity in this world or the next,

did not descend from Adam and Eve or any

origin story. My place is placeless, a trace

of the traceless. Neither body or soul.

I belong to the beloved, have seen the two

worlds as one and that one call to and know,

first, last, outer, inner, only that

breath breathing human being."

As we reflect on Rumi's teachings about the dance of opposites, we might ask ourselves: How can we embrace the paradoxes in our own lives? How might our perspective shift if we viewed apparent contradictions as complementary aspects of a greater whole? And how can we move beyond dualistic thinking to experience the unity that Rumi points to?

One of the most striking features of Rumi's poetry is his masterful use of paradox. Throughout his work, we encounter seemingly contradictory statements that, upon deeper reflection, reveal profound spiritual truths. This embrace of paradox is not mere literary device, but a reflection of Rumi's understanding of the nature of reality and the limitations of human perception.

As scholar Fatemeh Keshavarz notes in her book "Reading Mystical Lyric: The Case of Jalal al-Din Rumi" (1998), "Rumi's use of paradox serves to shatter our conventional modes of thinking, opening us to a reality that transcends logical categories."

One of Rumi's most famous paradoxical statements is (Rumi, The Essential Rumi):

"You are not a drop in the ocean.
You are the entire ocean in a drop."

This paradox challenges our usual sense of scale and identity. It suggests that our true nature is both infinitesimally small and infinitely vast, both individual and universal. It invites us to see ourselves not as separate entities, but as unique expressions of the divine whole.

Rumi frequently employs paradox to describe the nature of love and the relationship between lover and beloved (Rumi, The Essential Rumi):

"Love is the bridge between you and everything."

Here, love is portrayed as both a connection and a dissolution of boundaries. It is what links us to others and to the divine, yet in that linking, it erases the very sense of separation that makes a bridge necessary.

Another powerful paradox in Rumi's work is the idea of finding by losing (Rumi, The Essential Rumi):

"What you seek is seeking you."

This turns our usual understanding of spiritual seeking on its head. Instead of portraying the divine as something distant that we must strive to reach, Rumi suggests that it is already present, already seeking us. Our task is not to find God, but to realize that we have never been separate from God.

Rumi also uses paradox to express the ineffable nature of the divine (Rumi, The Essential Rumi):

"Silence is the language of God,

all else is poor translation."

Here, the paradox lies in using words to express the inadequacy of words. It points to a truth beyond language, inviting us into a direct experience that transcends conceptual understanding.

The theme of simultaneous emptiness and fullness is another paradox that recurs in Rumi's poetry (Rumi, The Essential Rumi):

"Empty yourself of everything.

Let the beauty of what you love be what you do."

This paradox suggests that true fullness comes through emptiness, that we must let go of our preconceptions and ego-attachments to be filled with divine presence.

Rumi's embrace of paradox extends to his view of spiritual practice. He often emphasizes the need for both effort and surrender:

"Knock, and He'll open the door.

Vanish, and He'll make you shine like the sun.

Fall, and He'll raise you to the heavens.

Become nothing, and He'll turn you into everything."

This paradoxical interplay between action and receptivity, doing and being, is at the heart of Rumi's spiritual teaching.

Even in his treatment of joy and sorrow, Rumi employs paradox (Rumi, The Essential Rumi):

"The wound is the place where the Light enters you."

This profound statement transforms our understanding of suffering, suggesting that our very vulnerability becomes the means of our illumination.

Rumi's use of paradox serves multiple purposes. It shakes us out of habitual patterns of thought, inviting us to see reality from a new perspective. It points to truths that cannot be captured in straightforward language. And it mirrors the paradoxical nature of the spiritual journey itself, where we must lose ourselves to find ourselves, die to be reborn, become empty to be filled.

As we contemplate these paradoxes, we're invited to hold seemingly contradictory truths in creative tension. We're challenged to move beyond either/or thinking into a both/and awareness that can contain the full richness of reality.

Rumi's paradoxes are not puzzles to be solved, but gateways to be entered. They invite us into a state of bewilderment that Rumi sees as essential to spiritual growth (Rumi, Masnavi):

"Sell your cleverness and buy bewilderment.

Cleverness is mere opinion, bewilderment is intuition."

This bewilderment is not confusion, but a state of openness and wonder in the face of mystery. It's a recognition of the limitations of our rational minds and an opening to a deeper, intuitive knowing.

As we continue our journey through "Mystic Ruminations," may we cultivate this spirit of paradox in our own lives. May we learn to embrace contradictions, to find unity in diversity, to see the infinite in the finite. For as Rumi reminds us (Rumi, The Essential Rumi):

"Out beyond ideas of wrongdoing and right doing,

there is a field. I'll meet you there."

In this field beyond duality, we may discover the ultimate paradox – that we are both distinct individuals and inseparable from the divine whole, both human and divine, both seekers and what we seek.

In the next chapter, we'll explore another key theme in Rumi's work: the use of nature as a mirror for spiritual truths.

A Community of the Spirit
There is a community of the spirit.
Join it, and feel the delight
of walking in the noisy street
and being the noise.
Drink all your passion,
and be a disgrace.
Close both eyes
to see with the other eye.
Open your hands,
if you want to be held.
Sit down in the circle.
Quit acting like a wolf, and feel
the shepherd's love filling you.
At night, your beloved wanders.
Don't accept consolations.
Close your mouth against food.
Taste the lover's mouth in yours.
You moan, "She left me." "He left me."
Twenty more will come.
Be empty of worrying.
Think of who created thought!
Why do you stay in prison
when the door is so wide open?
Move outside the tangle of fear-thinking.
Live in silence.
Flow down and down in always
widening rings of being.

This poem, often titled "A Community of the Spirit," beautifully illustrates many of the paradoxical themes discussed:

Unity of opposites: The poem begins by inviting us to be both "walking in the noisy street and being the noise," blurring the line between subject and object.

Transcending conventional morality: "Drink all your passion, and be a disgrace" echoes the text's discussion of moving beyond traditional notions of right and wrong.

Paradoxical instructions: "Close both eyes to see with the other eye" is a perfect example of Rumi's use of paradox to point to deeper truths.

Embracing contradictions: The poem contains many seemingly contradictory instructions, like "Open your hands, if you want to be held," which reflects Rumi's teaching about the interplay of opposites.

Finding fullness in emptiness: "Be empty of worrying. Think of who created thought!" touches on the theme of simultaneous emptiness and fullness mentioned in the text.

Transcending duality: The final lines, "Flow down and down in always widening rings of being," suggest a movement beyond individual identity into a wider, more encompassing reality.

The paradox of spiritual seeking: "Why do you stay in prison when the door is so wide open?" echoes the text's discussion of how what we seek is already present.

This poem, like much of Rumi's work, uses paradoxical language and imagery to shake us out of conventional thinking and point to a reality that transcends logical categories. It invites us to embrace contradictions, to find unity in diversity, and to move beyond our limited perceptions into a more expansive awareness.

The poem also reflects Rumi's teaching that spiritual truth often lies in the tension between opposites, rather than in choosing one side over the other. It challenges us to hold seemingly contradictory truths simultaneously, fostering a both/and awareness that can contain the full richness of reality.

Chapter 11: Nature as Mirror: Cosmic Metaphors

One of the most striking features of Rumi's poetry is his extensive use of natural imagery to convey spiritual truths. For Rumi, the natural world is not merely a backdrop for human affairs, but a living, breathing metaphor for the divine reality. This chapter will explore how Rumi uses elements of nature to illuminate the spiritual journey.

1. The Mirror of Creation

Rumi often portrays the natural world as a mirror reflecting divine attributes:

> "The beauty of the heart
> is the lasting beauty:
> its lips give to drink
> of the water of life."

Here, the human heart is likened to a wellspring, reflecting the life-giving nature of the divine.

2. The Wisdom of Plants

Plants, with their cycles of growth, dormancy, and rebirth, often serve as metaphors for spiritual transformation in Rumi's work (Rumi, The Essential Rumi):

> "The garden of the world has no limits,
> except in your mind.
> Its presence is more beautiful than the stars,
> with more clarity than the polished mirror of your heart."

The garden becomes a metaphor for the boundless potential of the soul.

3. Animal Wisdom

Rumi frequently uses animal behavior to illustrate spiritual principles (Rumi, The Essential Rumi):

> "You were born with potential.
> You were born with goodness and trust.
> You were born with ideals and dreams.
> You were born with greatness.
> You were born with wings.

You are not meant for crawling, so don't.
You have wings.
Learn to use them and fly."
Here, the contrast between crawling and flying becomes a powerful metaphor for spiritual awakening.

4. The Elements as Teachers

The four elements - earth, water, air, and fire - play a significant role in Rumi's metaphorical language:

"Water, stories, the body,

all the things we do, are mediums

that hide and show what's hidden.

Study them,

and enjoy this being washed

with a secret we sometimes know,

and then not."

Each element becomes a teacher, revealing different aspects of the spiritual journey.

5. Celestial Metaphors

The sun, moon, and stars are frequent players in Rumi's cosmic drama (Rumi, The Essential Rumi):

"The minute I heard my first love story,

I started looking for you, not knowing

how blind that was.

Lovers don't finally meet somewhere.

They're in each other all along."

Here, the search for the beloved is likened to the apparent movement of celestial bodies, which are, in reality, always present.

6. The Seasons of the Soul

Rumi often uses the changing seasons to illustrate the cycles of spiritual growth and transformation:

"Spring is Christ,

Raising martyred plants from their shrouds.

Their mouths open in gratitude, wanting to be kissed."

The rebirth of spring becomes a powerful metaphor for spiritual resurrection.

7. The Ocean of Unity

The ocean is a recurring metaphor in Rumi's work, often representing the vastness of divine reality (Rumi, The Essential Rumi):

"You are not a drop in the ocean.

You are the entire ocean in a drop."

This image beautifully captures the paradox of human existence - at once finite and infinite.

8. The Wind of Spirit

The invisible yet powerful wind often serves as a metaphor for the unseen workings of the divine:

"Where did the handsome beloved go?
I wonder, where did that tall, shapely cypress tree go?
He spread his light among us like a butterfly.
Why did he stop being a candle burning on this dark path?
Is there news from the friend who left and went away?
Are we still friends, or is this the end?
The wine gave us the gift of being our own master.
Why has the master of the tavern closed this wine-shop?
We are thirsty fish tossing in salty water.
Worshipper, come worship! Beloved, come back!
Return to the root of the root of your Self.
This world is filled with sunlight and love,
like motes of dust dancing in rays of sunlight."

Here, the wind becomes a metaphor for the beloved's presence, at once pervasive and elusive.

9. The Fire of Transformation

Fire, with its capacity to transform and purify, is a potent metaphor in Rumi's work (Rumi, The Essential Rumi):

> "Set your life on fire.
>
> Seek those who fan your flames."

The burning away of the false self in the fire of divine love is a central theme in Sufi thought, vividly brought to life in Rumi's verses.

10. The Book of Nature

Ultimately, for Rumi, the entire natural world is a book to be read, a text revealing divine wisdom:

> "The truth was a mirror in the hands of God.
>
> It fell, and broke into pieces.
>
> Everybody took a piece of it,
>
> and they looked at it and thought they had the truth."

This metaphor invites us to see beyond our limited perspectives and recognize the unity underlying all of creation.

As we reflect on Rumi's use of natural metaphors, we might ask ourselves: How can we cultivate a deeper awareness of the natural world as a mirror of spiritual realities? What wisdom might we glean from careful observation of nature's cycles and processes? And how might our relationship with the environment change if we saw it, as Rumi did, as a living text of divine revelation?

In the next chapter, we'll explore another central theme in Rumi's work: the transformative power of suffering and the alchemy of the soul.

The Sun Never Says
Even
After
All this time
The sun never says to the earth,
"You owe Me."
Look
What happens
With a love like that,
It lights the
Whole
Sky.

This poem, often titled "The Sun Never Says," beautifully illustrates Rumi's use of natural imagery to convey spiritual concepts:

The Sun as a Metaphor: The sun serves as a metaphor for divine love or the Divine itself. This reflects the text's mention of "Celestial Metaphors" where Rumi uses heavenly bodies to illustrate spiritual truths.

Unconditional Love: The sun's unconditional giving of light and warmth, without expecting anything in return, is a powerful metaphor for divine love and generosity. This aligns with the text's discussion of how Rumi sees nature as a mirror reflecting divine attributes.

Earth as Receiver: The earth, receiving the sun's light, can be seen as a metaphor for humanity or creation receiving divine love and grace.

Cosmic Scale: The poem uses the vast scale of the sun and sky to convey the immensity of divine love, echoing the text's mention of Rumi's "cosmic drama."

Transformative Power: The final lines about lighting the whole sky speak to the transformative power of unconditional love, reflecting the text's discussion of how Rumi uses natural phenomena to illustrate spiritual transformation.

Simplicity and Profundity: The poem's brevity and simplicity, combined with its profound message, exemplify Rumi's ability to use natural imagery to convey deep spiritual truths in an accessible way.

The Wisdom of Nature: By personifying the sun and earth, Rumi invites us to learn from nature's wisdom, as mentioned in the text's section on "The

Book of Nature."

This poem encapsulates Rumi's view of nature as a living text revealing divine wisdom. The poem also touches on themes of interconnectedness and the reciprocal relationship between different parts of creation, which are common in Rumi's work. It encourages us to consider how we might embody this kind of unconditional love in our own lives.

Chapter 12: The Alchemy of Suffering: Transforming Pain

One of the most profound and challenging aspects of Rumi's teachings is his perspective on suffering. Far from seeing pain and hardship as mere obstacles to be overcome, Rumi views them as essential catalysts for spiritual growth and transformation. This chapter will delve into Rumi's unique alchemy of suffering.

1. The Transformative Power of Pain

Rumi often speaks of suffering as a kind of spiritual furnace, refining the soul (Rumi, The Essential Rumi):

"The wound is the place where the Light enters you."

This perspective invites us to see our pain not as punishment, but as an opportunity for growth and illumination.

Rumi often speaks of suffering as a catalyst for spiritual growth [12]:

"The wound is the place where the Light enters you."

This perspective transforms our understanding of pain, suggesting that our very vulnerability becomes the means of our illumination.

2. Breaking the Ego

For Rumi, suffering often serves to break down the barriers of ego that separate us from the divine:

"You have to keep breaking your heart until it opens."

The shattering of our self-constructed identities becomes a doorway to a deeper, more authentic self.

3. The Night Journey

Rumi frequently uses the metaphor of darkness to represent periods of suffering or spiritual confusion (Rumi, The Essential Rumi):

"The moon stays bright when it doesn't avoid the night."

This imagery reminds us that times of darkness are not to be avoided, but embraced as part of the spiritual journey.

4. The Paradox of Healing

Rumi often points out the paradoxical nature of spiritual healing (Rumi, The Essential Rumi):

"The cure for pain is in the pain."

This suggests that by fully experiencing our suffering, rather than resisting it, we find the path to liberation.

5. Longing as a Spiritual Force

The pain of separation from the divine becomes, in Rumi's poetry, a powerful force for spiritual growth:

"Don't turn away. Keep your gaze on the bandaged place. That's where the light enters you."

This longing, or 'shauq' in Sufi terminology, is seen as evidence of our divine origin and destiny.

6. The Role of Difficulty in Spiritual Growth

Rumi frequently emphasizes the necessity of challenges for spiritual development:

"Difficulty is the name of an ancient tool that was created purely to help us define who we are."

This perspective invites us to welcome difficulties as opportunities for self-discovery and growth.

7. The Alchemy of Opposites

In Rumi's worldview, joy and sorrow, ease and difficulty, are not opposites to be chosen between, but complementary aspects of a greater whole:

"Sorrow prepares you for joy. It violently sweeps everything out of your house, so that new joy can find space to enter. It shakes the yellow leaves from the bough of your heart, so that fresh, green leaves can grow in their place."

8. Surrender as the Key

For Rumi, the key to transforming suffering lies in surrender:

"When I run after what I think I want, my days are a furnace of stress and anxiety; if I sit in my own place of patience, what I need flows to me, and without pain. From this I understand that what I want also wants me, is looking for me and attracting me."

This surrender is not passive resignation, but an active alignment with the flow of existence.

9. The Polishing of the Mirror

Rumi often uses the metaphor of polishing a mirror to describe the process of spiritual purification through suffering:

"Your depression is connected to your insolence and refusal to praise. Praise is the polish; it is the cleanser for your mirror. If you wish to be free of your own ugly wax, you must melt yourself in praise."

10. The Path of Love

Ultimately, for Rumi, all suffering is transformed through love:

"Through love all pain will turn to medicine."

Love becomes the ultimate alchemical agent, transmuting the lead of suffering into the gold of spiritual realization.

11. The Cosmic Dance

Rumi often portrays the interplay of joy and sorrow as a cosmic dance (Rumi, The Essential Rumi):

"Dance, when you're broken open. Dance, if you've torn the bandage off. Dance in the middle of the fighting. Dance in your blood. Dance when you're perfectly free."

This image invites us to participate fully in life, embracing both its sorrows and its joys.

12. The Goal of Suffering

For Rumi, the ultimate purpose of suffering is to lead us back to our divine origin:

"The pain you feel is the distance between what you are and what you can be."

As we reflect on Rumi's teachings about the alchemy of suffering, we might ask ourselves: How can we embrace our pain as a catalyst for growth? What might change in our lives if we viewed difficulties as opportunities rather than obstacles? And how can we cultivate the love that Rumi speaks of, which has the power to transform all suffering?

In the next chapter, we'll explore another central theme in Rumi's work: the symbolism of intoxication and the concept of spiritual ecstasy.

The Wound of Love

I saw grief drinking a cup of sorrow
and called out,
"It tastes sweet, does it not?"
"You've caught me," grief answered,
"and you've ruined my business.
How can I sell sorrow,
when you know it's a blessing?"
I saw the healing process commencing,
and the wound turning into a rose.
I saw how yesterday and today are
the same.
I saw how fleeting life is,
and how no one can remain.
I saw that the wine
which brings joy to the soul
pours from the heart and the eyes.

I saw that all things
are a new creation every moment,
and that nothing stays the same.
I saw the secret of eternal life
in the depths of each breath.
I saw how love
beautifies every being,
and I saw the face of my Beloved
in every face.

This poem beautifully illustrates many of the themes discussed in the text about Rumi's perspective on suffering and transformation:

The sweetness in sorrow: The opening lines reflect Rumi's view that suffering can be a "blessing" or opportunity for growth, not just a negative experience.

Transformation of pain: "The wound turning into a rose" directly echoes the text's discussion of Rumi seeing pain as a catalyst for spiritual growth.

Impermanence: The lines about fleeting life and constant change reflect the text's mention of breaking the ego and the transformative power of suffering.

Love as the ultimate transformer: The final stanza, especially "I saw how love beautifies every being," aligns with the text's point about love being the ultimate alchemical agent in Rumi's philosophy.

Unity in diversity: Seeing "the face of my Beloved in every face" reflects the text's discussion of Rumi's view of the interconnectedness of all experiences and beings.

The present moment: The emphasis on each moment being a new creation echoes the text's point about Rumi encouraging full participation in life's experiences.

Breath as life: The line about "the secret of eternal life in the depths of each breath" could be seen as a reference to surrender and alignment with existence, which the text mentions as key to Rumi's approach to suffering.

This poem encapsulates Rumi's perspective on suffering as a transformative force. It presents a journey from recognizing the value in sorrow, through understanding impermanence, to ultimately seeing love and the divine in all things. The poem invites us to shift our perspective on pain and difficulty, viewing them not as obstacles but as part of a larger process of spiritual growth and realization.

The poem's structure, moving from specific observations to more universal truths, mirrors the spiritual journey itself - from individual experiences of pain and joy to a broader understanding of life's interconnectedness and the omnipresence of love.

Chapter 13: Mystical Intoxication: Symbolism of Wine

One of the most captivating and controversial aspects of Rumi's poetry is his frequent use of wine and intoxication as metaphors for spiritual experience. In this chapter, we'll explore the rich symbolism of mystical intoxication in Rumi's work and its deeper spiritual implications.

1. The Wine of Divine Love

In Rumi's poetry, wine often symbolizes divine love and spiritual ecstasy: "Drink wine. This is life eternal. This is all that youth will give you. It is the season for wine, roses and drunken friends. Be happy for this moment. This moment is your life."

Here, the intoxication of wine becomes a metaphor for the all-consuming nature of divine love.

2. The Tavern of Unity

Rumi often speaks of a spiritual tavern, a place where the seeker can drink deeply of divine presence:

"In the tavern of mystics, there is a wine for every soul."

This tavern symbolizes a state of consciousness where individual identity dissolves into unity with the divine.

3. The Cupbearer as Divine Guide

The figure of the cupbearer, or saqi, is a recurring character in Rumi's poetry, often representing the spiritual guide or the divine itself:

"Last night, I was lying on the rooftop, thinking of you. I saw a special Star, and summoned her to take you a message. I prostrated myself to the Star and asked her to take my prostration to that Sun of Tabriz. I opened my chest and showed her my scars, I told her to bring me news of my Beloved. I waited and waited, until the Star set and dawn broke, and here I am, still waiting for the answer."

4. Sobriety vs. Spiritual Drunkenness

Rumi often contrasts ordinary sobriety with spiritual intoxication:

"Be drunk with love, for love is all that exists."

In this context, sobriety represents the limited perspective of the ego, while drunkenness symbolizes a state of divine union.

5. The Hangover of Separation

Just as Rumi speaks of spiritual intoxication, he also describes the pain of separation from the divine in terms of a hangover:

> "I am so drunk I have lost the way in
> and the way out.
> I have lost the earth, the moon, and the sky.
> Don't put another cup of wine in my hand,
> pour it in my mouth,
> for I have lost the way to my mouth."

6. The Grape's Journey

Rumi sometimes uses the journey of the grape - from vine to wine - as a metaphor for the soul's transformation:

> "I was raw, I became cooked, I was burnt."

This process of transformation through love is central to Rumi's spiritual teachings.

7. Breaking the Jug

The breaking of the wine jug is another powerful image in Rumi's poetry, often symbolizing the shattering of the ego:

> "Break the jug of your ego, spill the wine of your self."

8. The Forbidden Drink

Rumi often plays with the idea of wine as a forbidden substance, using this tension to highlight the countercultural nature of the mystical path:

> "Whoever has been taught the secrets of love
> should wash his hands of piety and religion."

9. The Universal Intoxicant

For Rumi, the intoxication of divine love is not limited to any particular faith or practice:

> "I am neither Christian, nor Jewish, nor Muslim. I am not of the East, nor of the West... I have put duality away, I have seen the two worlds as one; One I seek, One I know, One I see, One I call."

10. Beyond Metaphor

While Rumi's wine symbolism is generally understood metaphorically, he sometimes suggests that the spiritual intoxication he speaks of is more real than physical drunkenness:

> "Those who don't feel this Love

pulling them like a river,
those who don't drink dawn
like a cup of spring water
or take in sunset like supper,
those who don't want to change,
let them sleep."

11. The Eternal Tavern

Rumi often speaks of an eternal tavern, a realm beyond time and space where the soul can drink deeply of divine presence (Rumi, The Essential Rumi):

"Out beyond ideas of wrongdoing and rightdoing,
there is a field. I'll meet you there.
When the soul lies down in that grass,
the world is too full to talk about.
Ideas, language, even the phrase 'each other'
doesn't make any sense."

12. The Ultimate Intoxication

Ultimately, for Rumi, the goal is not just momentary experiences of spiritual ecstasy, but a permanent state of divine intoxication:

"Gamble everything for love,
if you are a true human being.
If not, leave this gathering.
Half-heartedness doesn't reach into majesty."

As we reflect on Rumi's symbolism of mystical intoxication, we might ask ourselves: What in our lives intoxicates us with joy and meaning? How can we cultivate a deeper 'drunkenness' with divine love? And how might our perspective shift if we viewed our spiritual journey as a process of progressive intoxication with the divine?

In our final thematic chapter, we'll explore Rumi's teachings on silence and sound, and the music of the soul.

A Great Wagon

Out beyond ideas of wrongdoing and rightdoing,
there is a field. I'll meet you there.
When the soul lies down in that grass,
the world is too full to talk about.
Ideas, language, even the phrase "each other"

doesn't make any sense.
The breeze at dawn has secrets to tell you.
Don't go back to sleep.
You must ask for what you really want.
Don't go back to sleep.
People are going back and forth across the doorsill
where the two worlds touch.
The door is round and open.
Don't go back to sleep.
I would love to kiss you.
The price of kissing is your life.
Now my loving is running toward my life shouting,
What a bargain, let's buy it.
Daylight, full of small dancing particles
and the one great turning, our souls
are dancing with you, without feet, they dance.
Can you see them when I whisper in your ear?
All day and night, music,
a quiet, bright
reedsong. If it
fades, we fade.

This poem, often titled "A Great Wagon," beautifully illustrates many of the themes discussed in the text about Rumi's use of intoxication as a spiritual metaphor:

The Tavern of Unity: The "field" beyond wrongdoing and rightdoing can be seen as analogous to the spiritual tavern mentioned in the text, a place of unity and transcendence.

Mystical Intoxication: The imagery of the soul lying down in the grass and the world being "too full to talk about" evokes a state of spiritual intoxication or ecstasy.

Beyond Ordinary Consciousness: The repeated refrain "Don't go back to sleep" echoes the text's discussion of spiritual drunkenness as a heightened state of awareness.

Divine Love: The lines about kissing and the bargain of giving one's life for love reflect the text's emphasis on divine love as the ultimate intoxicant.

Universal Intoxication: The image of souls dancing without feet speaks to the universal nature of this spiritual ecstasy, transcending physical limitations.

Music and Intoxication: The final stanza's mention of music connects to the text's discussion of the relationship between spiritual intoxication and divine melodies.

The Eternal Tavern: The poem's depiction of a timeless, boundless state where ordinary concepts lose meaning aligns with the text's mention of an "eternal tavern" beyond time and space.

This poem encapsulates Rumi's use of intoxication as a spiritual metaphor, inviting the reader into a state of heightened awareness and unity with the divine. It challenges us to move beyond our ordinary perceptions and to remain "awake" to the deeper realities of existence.

The poem's structure, with its mix of imagery and direct exhortations, mirrors the experience of spiritual intoxication itself - at once vivid and elusive, inviting and challenging. It encourages us to fully engage with life, to seek out the "secrets" that the world has to tell us, and to be willing to pay the price (our limited sense of self) for the kiss of divine union.

Chapter 14: Silence and Sound: The Music of the Soul

In Rumi's poetry and teachings, the interplay between silence and sound holds a special significance. This chapter will explore how Rumi uses these concepts to illuminate the spiritual journey and the nature of the divine.

1. The Power of Silence

Rumi often speaks of silence as a gateway to deeper spiritual understanding (Rumi, The Essential Rumi):

"Silence is the language of God,

all else is poor translation."

For Rumi, true silence is not merely the absence of sound, but a state of receptivity to divine presence.

2. The Song of the Reed Flute

One of Rumi's most famous metaphors is that of the reed flute, separated from its reed bed:

"Listen to the story told by the reed,

of being separated.

Since I was cut from the reedbed,

I have made this crying sound."

The haunting music of the flute becomes a metaphor for the soul's longing for its divine origin.

3. The Cosmic Symphony

Rumi often describes the universe itself as a kind of divine music:

"We have fallen into the place

where everything is music."

This perspective invites us to attune ourselves to the harmony underlying all of existence.

4. The Dance of Silence and Sound

For Rumi, silence and sound are not opposites, but complementary aspects of a greater whole:

"In silence there is eloquence. Stop weaving and see how the pattern improves."

This interplay between silence and sound mirrors the dance between stillness and movement in spiritual practice.

5. The Inner Music

Rumi speaks of an inner music that can only be heard when external noise ceases:

> "All day and night, music,
> a quiet, bright
> reedsong. If it
> fades, we fade."

This inner music is closely associated with the voice of the divine within.

6. Words as Veils

While Rumi was a master of words, he often points out their limitations:

> "Words are a pretext. It is the inner bond that draws one person to another, not words."

This paradoxical use of words to point beyond words is a hallmark of Rumi's poetry.

7. The Sama Ceremony

The whirling dance of the Mevlevi dervishes, which Rumi is said to have originated, is a powerful embodiment of the interplay between silence and sound (Rumi, The Essential Rumi):

> "In your light I learn how to love.
> In your beauty, how to make poems.
> You dance inside my chest where no one sees you,
> but sometimes I do, and that sight becomes this art."

8. The Silence Beyond Words

Rumi often points to a silence that is not merely the absence of sound, but a profound presence (Rumi, The Essential Rumi):

> "There is a voice that doesn't use words. Listen."

This silence is closely associated with the state of fana, or annihilation in the divine.

9. The Music of the Spheres

Drawing on ancient Greek and Islamic concepts, Rumi sometimes refers to the music of the celestial spheres:

> "The sky is a suspended blue ocean.
> The stars are the fish that swim."

This cosmic music becomes a metaphor for the divine harmony underlying all of creation.

10. The Heart's Ear

Rumi often speaks of a special faculty of spiritual hearing:

> "What is the deep listening? Sama is
> a greeting from the secret ones inside
> the heart, a letter."

This inner hearing allows one to perceive spiritual realities beyond the reach of ordinary senses.

11. The Ecstatic Utterance

While Rumi values silence, he also celebrates ecstatic utterance as an expression of divine love:

> "I want to sing like the birds sing, not worrying about who hears or what they think."

This kind of speech, born of spiritual intoxication, transcends ordinary communication.

12. The Ultimate Silence

Ultimately, for Rumi, the highest state is one that transcends both silence and sound (Rumi, The Essential Rumi):

> "Out beyond ideas of wrongdoing and rightdoing,
> there is a field. I'll meet you there.
> When the soul lies down in that grass,
> the world is too full to talk about."

This state of unity goes beyond all dualities, including that of silence and sound.

As we reflect on Rumi's teachings about silence and sound, we might ask ourselves: How can we cultivate a deeper inner silence in our lives? What is the music that our souls long to express? And how can we attune ourselves to the cosmic symphony that Rumi describes?

Where Everything is Music
Don't worry about saving these songs!
And if one of our instruments breaks,
it doesn't matter.
We have fallen into the place
where everything is music.
The strumming and the flute notes
rise into the atmosphere,
and even if the whole world's harp
should burn up, there will still be
hidden instruments playing.
So the candle flickers and goes out.
We have a piece of flint, and a spark.
This singing art is sea foam.
The graceful movements come from a pearl
somewhere on the ocean floor.
Poems reach up like spindrift and the edge
of driftwood along the beach, wanting!
They derive
from a slow and powerful root
that we can't see.
Stop the words now.
Open the window in the center of your chest,
and let the spirits fly in and out.

This poem, often titled "Where Everything is Music," beautifully illustrates many of the themes discussed in the text about Rumi's perspective on silence, sound, and the music of the soul:

The Cosmic Symphony: The line "We have fallen into the place where everything is music" directly echoes the text's mention of Rumi describing the universe as a divine music.

Inner Music: The reference to "hidden instruments playing" even if the world's harp burns up aligns with the text's discussion of an inner music that can be heard when external noise ceases.

Beyond Physical Instruments: The poem's dismissal of worry about saving songs or broken instruments reflects Rumi's focus on a music that transcends physical sound.

The Power of Silence: The final lines, "Stop the words now. Open the window in the center of your chest," evoke the text's discussion of silence as a gateway to deeper spiritual understanding.

The Heart's Ear: The imagery of letting "spirits fly in and out" of the chest suggests the special faculty of spiritual hearing mentioned in the text.

Words as Veils: The command to "Stop the words now" at the end of the poem reflects the text's point about Rumi acknowledging the limitations of words.

The Dance of Silence and Sound: The poem's movement between descriptions of music and calls for silence mirrors the text's discussion of the interplay between silence and sound in Rumi's work.

This poem encapsulates Rumi's view of a universe infused with divine music, both audible and inaudible. It invites us to tune into a deeper, subtler level of reality where everything is indeed music. The poem also reflects Rumi's teaching that true spirituality involves moving beyond external forms (like instruments or words) to a direct experience of the divine harmony underlying all existence.

The structure of the poem, with its mix of vivid imagery and direct exhortations, mirrors the experience of spiritual listening itself - at once richly sensory and profoundly silent. It encourages us to open ourselves to the music of the universe, while also cultivating the inner silence necessary to truly hear it.

Part IV: Enchanted Conversations - A Treasury of Rumi's Poetry

Chapter 15: Songs of Longing

1. "The Guest House"

This being human is a guest house.
Every morning a new arrival.
A joy, a depression, a meanness,
some momentary awareness comes
as an unexpected visitor.
Welcome and entertain them all!
Even if they're a crowd of sorrows,
who violently sweep your house
empty of its furniture,
still, treat each guest honorably.
He may be clearing you out
for some new delight.
The dark thought, the shame, the malice,
meet them at the door laughing,
and invite them in.
Be grateful for whoever comes,
because each has been sent
as a guide from beyond.

Commentary: This poem beautifully encapsulates Rumi's philosophy of embracing all of life's experiences, both pleasant and unpleasant. The metaphor of the guest house invites us to view our emotions and experiences as temporary visitors, each bringing its own lesson or gift. The poem encourages a radical acceptance and even gratitude for all that life brings, seeing each experience as a potential teacher or "guide from beyond."

2. "Love Dogs"

One night a man was crying,
Allah! Allah!
His lips grew sweet with the praising,
until a cynic said,
"So! I have heard you
calling out, but have you ever

gotten any response?"
The man had no answer to that.
He quit praying and fell into a confused sleep.
He dreamed he saw Khidr, the guide of souls,
in a thick, green foliage.
"Why did you stop praising?"
"Because I've never heard anything back."
"This longing
you express is the return message."
The grief you cry out from
draws you toward union.
Your pure sadness
that wants help
is the secret cup.
Listen to the moan of a dog for its master.
That whining is the connection.
There are love dogs
no one knows the names of.
Give your life
to be one of them.

Commentary: This poem speaks to the power of longing and devotion. The cynical question about the lack of response to prayer is met with a profound answer: the longing itself is the response. Rumi suggests that our very desire for connection with the divine is evidence of that connection. The image of the dog's devotion to its master beautifully illustrates this idea of unconditional love and longing.

3. "A Moment of Happiness"

A moment of happiness,
you and I sitting on the verandah,
apparently two, but one in soul, you and I.
We feel the flowing water of life here,
you and I, with the garden's beauty
and the birds singing.
The stars will be watching us,
and we will show them

what it is to be a thin crescent moon.
You and I unselfed, will be together,
indifferent to idle speculation, you and I.
The parrots of heaven will be cracking sugar
as we laugh together, you and I.
In one form upon this earth,
and in another form in a timeless sweet land.

Commentary: This poem beautifully captures the ecstasy of union with the beloved, whether understood as a human lover or the divine. The repetition of "you and I" emphasizes the theme of unity in duality. The imagery of nature - the garden, birds, stars, and moon - places this moment of communion within the context of the entire cosmos, suggesting that true love aligns us with the harmony of the universe.

4. "The Ocean of Unity"

"In the depths of my being, I found an ocean,
Vast and boundless, without motion.
Every drop contains the whole,
In each atom, I saw your soul.
Waves may rise and fall on the surface,
But in the depths, there's only your embrace.
I am not this body, nor this mind,
But the eternal love, impossible to define."

Commentary: This poem explores the Sufi concept of wahdat al-wujud (unity of existence). The ocean metaphor represents the divine reality, while the waves symbolize the temporary forms of the manifest world. The poem suggests that our true nature is this all-encompassing divine love, beyond individual identity.

5. "The Dance of Existence"

"Whirling, twirling, in endless motion,
Atoms dance in cosmic devotion.
In every spin, in every turn,
The secrets of the universe we learn.
Like a dervish, lost in ecstasy,
We move to a divine melody.
In this dance of love, we disappear,

And the Beloved's face becomes clear."

Commentary: This poem draws inspiration from the Sufi practice of sama, or whirling meditation. It portrays existence itself as a divine dance, with every particle in the universe moving in harmony with the divine will. The dissolution of the self in this cosmic dance represents the mystical state of fana, or annihilation in God.

6. "The Mirror of the Heart"

"Polish the mirror of your heart, my friend,
For in its reflection, all dualities end.
Lover and beloved, self and other,
In this mirror, discover your true lover.
The dust of ego clouds your sight,
Wipe it clean with love's pure light.
In the clarity of this reflection,
Find the source of all perfection."

Commentary: This poem uses the metaphor of a mirror to represent the human heart. In Sufi tradition, the heart is seen as the site of divine revelation. The poem encourages spiritual purification, removing the "dust" of ego and worldly attachments to reveal the divine reality within.

7. "The Tavern of Eternity"

"In the tavern of eternity, I drank the wine,
That made all moments divine.
Past and future dissolved away,
In the eternal now, I chose to stay.
The cupbearer filled my glass to the brim,
With love that made my senses swim.
Drunk on the beauty of the Friend,
I found a bliss that knows no end."

Commentary: This poem employs the common Sufi metaphor of spiritual intoxication. The "tavern of eternity" represents the realm of mystical experience, while the wine symbolizes divine love. The dissolution of past and future points to the timeless nature of spiritual realization.

8. "The Alchemy of Love"'

"In the crucible of the heart,
The lead of self transforms to art.
With love's fire, intense and bright,
The soul turns to pure light.
This alchemy, oh so divine,
Turns water into the finest wine.
In love's embrace, all is made new,
And many are transformed to One True."

Commentary: This poem draws on alchemical imagery to describe the transformative power of divine love. The process of spiritual purification is likened to the alchemical transformation of base metals into gold. The poem suggests that divine love has the power to transmute the lower aspects of our nature into spiritual gold.

These poems and their commentaries offer a glimpse into the mystical worldview of Sufism, as inspired by Rumi's teachings. They explore themes of unity, spiritual transformation, divine intoxication, and the primacy of love in the spiritual journey. Like Rumi's own works, these poems invite the reader to look beyond the surface of reality and to recognize the divine presence permeating all of existence.

These poems offer a glimpse into Rumi's profound understanding of love and longing. In the next chapter, we'll explore poems that speak to the theme of spiritual awakening and transformation.

Chapter 16: Hymns of Union

In this chapter, we'll explore poems that speak to the experience of spiritual union and the dissolution of the self in the divine.

1. "Only Breath"

Not Christian or Jew or Muslim, not Hindu
Buddhist, sufi, or zen. Not any religion
or cultural system. I am not from the East
or the West, not out of the ocean or up
from the ground, not natural or ethereal, not
composed of elements at all. I do not exist,
am not an entity in this world or the next,
did not descend from Adam and Eve or any
origin story. My place is placeless, a trace
of the traceless. Neither body or soul.
I belong to the beloved, have seen the two
worlds as one and that one call to and know,
first, last, outer, inner, only that
breath breathing human being.

Commentary: This poem powerfully expresses the state of complete union with the divine, where all dualities and distinctions dissolve. Rumi systematically negates all forms of identity - religious, cultural, physical, metaphysical - to point to a state of being that transcends all categories. The final line, referring to "that breath breathing human being," suggests that our true essence is simply the divine breath flowing through us.

2. "The Drum of the Realization"

Why are you so enchanted by this world
when a mine of gold lies within you?
Open your eyes and come—-
Return to the root of the root of your own soul.
You have been a prisoner of a little pond,
I am the ocean and its turbulent flood.
Come merge with me,
leave this world of ignorance.

Be with me, I will open the gate to your love.
Come, come, whoever you are.
Wanderer, worshiper, lover of leaving.
It doesn't matter.
Ours is not a caravan of despair.
Come, even if you have broken your vows
a thousand times.
Come, yet again, come, come.

Commentary: This poem is a passionate call to awakening and union. The metaphor of the gold mine within speaks to the inherent divine nature of the human soul. The contrast between the "little pond" and the "ocean" emphasizes the limitless nature of divine reality compared to our limited ego-consciousness. The final stanza, with its famous refrain "Come, come, whoever you are," is a beautiful expression of the inclusive and unconditional nature of divine love.

3. "The Essence of Desire"

All through eternity
Beauty unveils His exquisite form
in the solitude of nothingness;
He holds a mirror to His Face
and beholds His own beauty.
he is the knower and the known,
the seer and the seen;
No eye but His own
has ever looked upon this Universe.
His every quality finds an expression:
Eternity becomes the verdant field of Time and Space;
Love, the life-giving garden of this world.
Every branch and leaf and fruit
Reveals an aspect of His perfection-
They cypress gives hint of His grace,
The rose gives tidings of His beauty.
Whenever Beauty looks,
Love is also there;
Whenever beauty shows a rosy cheek
Love lights Her fire from that flame.
When beauty dwells in the dark folds of night
Love comes and finds a heart
entangled in tresses.
Beauty and Love are as body and soul.
Beauty is the mine, Love is the diamond.
They have together
since the beginning of time-
Side by side, step by step.

Commentary: This poem offers a profound vision of the nature of existence as an expression of divine beauty and love. The image of God beholding His own beauty in the mirror of creation is a classic Sufi concept. The poem suggests that all of existence - time, space, nature - is an expression of divine attributes. The interplay between beauty and love is portrayed as the fundamental dynamic of the universe.

These poems offer deep insights into the Sufi understanding of union with the divine. They invite us to look beyond our limited identities, to recognize our inherent divine nature, and to see all of existence as an expression of divine beauty and love.

In the next chapter, we'll explore poems that celebrate the beloved in its various forms - human, divine, and the blurring of lines between the two.

Chapter 17: Odes to the Beloved

In this chapter, we'll explore poems that celebrate the beloved in its various manifestations - human, divine, and the mysterious interplay between the two.

1. "The Sunrise Ruby"

In the early morning hour,
just before dawn, lover and beloved wake
and take a drink of water.
She asks, "Do you love me or yourself more?
Really, tell the absolute truth."
He says, "There's nothing left of me.
I'm like a ruby held up to the sunrise.
Is it still a stone, or a world
made of redness? It has no resistance
to sunlight."
This is how Hallaj said, I am God,
and told the truth!
The ruby and the sunrise are one.
Be courageous and discipline yourself.
Completely become hearing and ear,
and wear this sun-ruby as an earring.
Work. Keep digging your well.
Don't think about getting off from work.
Water is there somewhere.
Submit to a daily practice.
Your loyalty to that
is a ring on the door.
Keep knocking, and the joy inside
will eventually open a window
and look out to see who's there.

Commentary: This poem beautifully illustrates the Sufi concept of fana, or annihilation of the self in the divine. The metaphor of the ruby held up to the sunrise suggests a state of complete transparency and union with the divine light. The reference to Hallaj, a famous Sufi martyr who was executed for declaring "I am God," underscores the radical nature of this union. The poem also emphasizes the importance of spiritual practice and perseverance in attaining this state.

2. "Who Says Words with My Mouth?"

All day I think about it, then at night I say it.
Where did I come from, and what am I supposed to be doing?
I have no idea.
My soul is from elsewhere, I'm sure of that,
and I intend to end up there.
This drunkenness began in some other tavern.
When I get back around to that place,
I'll be completely sober. Meanwhile,
I'm like a bird from another continent, sitting in this aviary.
The day is coming when I fly off,
but who is it now in my ear who hears my voice?
Who says words with my mouth?
Who looks out with my eyes? What is the soul?
I cannot stop asking.
If I could taste one sip of an answer,
I could break out of this prison for drunks.
I didn't come here of my own accord, and I can't leave that way.
Whoever brought me here will have to take me home.
This poetry. I never know what I'm going to say.
I don't plan it.
When I'm outside the saying of it,
I get very quiet and rarely speak at all.

Commentary: This poem expresses the profound spiritual questioning that characterizes the Sufi path. The speaker's sense of being from "elsewhere" and the metaphor of being a bird from another continent capture the feeling of not belonging fully to this world. The questions about the nature of the self and the soul reflect the Sufi's constant inquiry into the nature of reality. The final stanza, describing the spontaneous nature of the poetry, suggests that true spiritual expression comes not from the individual ego but from a deeper source.

3. "The Meaning of Love"

Both light and shadow

are the dance of Love.
Love has no cause;
it is the astrolabe of God's secrets.
Lover and Loving are inseparable
and timeless.
Although I may try to describe Love
when I experience it I am speechless.
Although I may try to write about Love
I am rendered helpless;
my pen breaks and the paper slips away
at the ineffable place
where Lover, Loving and Loved are one.
Every moment is made glorious
by the light of Love.

Commentary: This poem explores the ineffable nature of divine love. The metaphor of the astrolabe, an ancient astronomical instrument, suggests that love is the means by which we can understand the mysteries of the divine. The poem emphasizes the unity of lover, beloved, and the act of loving, pointing to a state beyond duality. The final stanza suggests that love is not just a feeling or an action, but the very essence of existence, glorifying every moment.

These poems offer profound insights into the Sufi understanding of love and the beloved. They invite us to see love not just as a human emotion, but as the fundamental reality of existence, and to recognize the beloved in all its forms - human, divine, and the mysterious space where the two merge.

In the next chapter, we'll explore poems that delve into the theme of spiritual intoxication and ecstasy.

Chapter 18: Ghazals of Spiritual Intoxication

In this chapter, we'll explore poems that delve into the theme of spiritual intoxication and ecstasy, a central concept in Sufi poetry.

1. "The Tavern"

I am so small I can barely be seen.

How can this great love be inside me?

Look at your eyes. They are small,

but they see enormous things.

Open your heart and listen to the mysterious music.

Can you hear it? It's coming from the tavern.

Let's go there and get drunk on love.

The wine is ready, the tavern open.

I have seen the eternal tavern-keeper,

inviting us all to come in.

He says, "Why are you standing there like a beggar?

Come in, you are the king of this tavern."

We are the mirror as well as the face in it.

We are tasting the taste this minute

of eternity. We are pain

and what cures pain, both. We are

the sweet cold water and the jar that pours.

Commentary: This ghazal uses the metaphor of intoxication and the tavern to describe the experience of divine love. The contrast between the smallness of the individual and the greatness of love echoes the Sufi concept of the human heart containing the infinite divine. The tavern represents the realm of spiritual experience, where conventional distinctions dissolve and one experiences unity with the divine.

2. "The Wine of Love"

Our master has gone mad!

He has torn off his robe and run into the wilderness.

He is drunk with the wine of love,

staggering and reeling like a whirling dervish.

The wine of love is headier than all other wines.

It makes the sober drunk and the drunk sober.
It turns lions into foxes and foxes into lions.
It makes the bitter sweet and the sweet bitter.
Bring more wine, O cupbearer!
Fill our cups to the brim.
Let us drink until we forget
who is the lover and who the beloved.
In this tavern, there is no difference
between the king and the beggar.
All are drunk with the same wine,
all are beggars at love's door.

Commentary: This poem celebrates the intoxicating and transformative power of divine love. The image of the master going mad and running into the wilderness represents the way spiritual ecstasy can appear irrational to the uninitiated. The paradoxical effects of this "wine" - making the sober drunk and the drunk sober - point to the way spiritual realization can overturn conventional understanding.

3. "The Drunkard's Song"

I am so drunk I have lost the way in
and the way out.
I have lost the earth, the moon, and the sky.
Don't put another cup of wine in my hand,
pour it in my mouth,
for I have lost the way to my mouth.
I am blown like smoke from a flame.
I am a bubble floating in the wind.
I am a star thrown down from the sky.
I am a bird made of fire, flying without wings.
The sea is foaming at the mouth:
it's looking for me, it wants to swallow me.
The desert is running away:
it's afraid I will turn it into a garden.
My secrets are written on leaves in the garden.
But the wind comes and blows them away.
If you want to read them, hurry!

For I am drunk and about to fall asleep.

Commentary: This poem vividly describes the state of spiritual intoxication. The loss of ordinary faculties and orientation represents the dissolution of the ego in mystical experience. The surreal imagery - being blown like smoke, a bubble in the wind, a wingless bird of fire - conveys the sense of transcendence and transformation. The urgency in the final stanza suggests the ephemeral nature of mystical insights.

These poems offer a taste of the ecstatic dimension of Sufi spirituality. They invite us to move beyond our ordinary state of consciousness and experience the intoxicating presence of the divine.

In our next chapter, we'll explore Rumi's quatrains, which often distill profound wisdom into just a few lines.

Chapter 19: Quatrains of Wisdom

Rumi's quatrains, known as rubaiyat, are short, four-line poems that often pack profound spiritual insights into a compact form. Here's a selection of some of his most impactful quatrains:

1. "The Seeker's Path"

"Sell your cleverness and buy bewilderment.

Cleverness is mere opinion, bewilderment is intuition.

Let yourself be silently drawn by the strange pull of what you really love.

It will not lead you astray."

Commentary: This quatrain encapsulates Rumi's emphasis on intuitive wisdom over intellectual knowledge. The contrast between "cleverness" and "bewilderment" suggests that true understanding comes not from rational analysis, but from a state of openness and wonder.

2. "The Mirror of the Heart"

"Your task is not to seek for love,

but merely to seek and find all the barriers within yourself

that you have built against it.

Love is the water of life. And a lover is a soul of fire!"

Commentary: This quatrain beautifully expresses Rumi's understanding of love as our essential nature, rather than something to be sought externally. The metaphor of love as water and the lover as fire creates a powerful image of transformation.

3. "The Dance of Existence"

"We came whirling out of nothingness,

scattering stars like dust.

The stars made a circle,

and in the middle, we dance."

Commentary: This quatrain paints a cosmic picture of existence, with human consciousness as a dance at the center of the universe. It suggests both our insignificance in the grand scheme and our central role in the cosmic drama.

4. "The Wound of Love"

"The wound is the place where the Light enters you.

Don't turn away.

Keep looking at the bandaged place.

That's where the light enters you."

Commentary: This quatrain transforms the concept of suffering, suggesting that our wounds and vulnerabilities are actually openings for spiritual growth and illumination.

5. "The Ocean of Being"

"You are not a drop in the ocean.

You are the entire ocean in a drop.

Look inside yourself;

everything that you want, you already are."

Commentary: This quatrain expresses the Sufi concept of wahdat al-wujud, or the unity of existence. It suggests that each individual contains within themselves the entirety of divine reality.

6. "The Power of Now"

"Past and future veil God from our sight;

Burn up both of them with fire.

How long will you be partitioned by these segments?

How long will you stay in the shape you have taken?"

Commentary: This quatrain emphasizes the importance of presence and transcending linear time. It suggests that our attachment to past and future obscures our perception of divine reality.

7. "The Paradox of Seeking"

"I searched for God among the Christians and on the Cross and therein I found Him not.

I went into the ancient temples of idolatry; no trace of Him was there.

I entered the mountain cave of Hira and then went as far as Qandhar but God I found not.

Then I directed my search to the Kaaba, the resort of old and young; God was not there even.

Finally, I looked into my own heart and there I saw Him; He was nowhere else."

Commentary: This longer quatrain (expanded to more lines) describes the futility of seeking God in external forms and places. It concludes with the fundamental Sufi teaching that the divine is to be found within one's own heart.17

8. "The Silence of Love"

> "Lovers don't finally meet somewhere.
> They're in each other all along.
> The moment I heard my first love story,
> I started looking for you, not knowing how blind that was."

Commentary: This quatrain expresses the Sufi concept that lover and beloved are ultimately one. It suggests that the journey of seeking is a process of recognizing what has always been present.

9. "The Veil of Separation"

> "A gossamer veil, thin as a breath,
> Separates me from my Beloved's face.
> With each heartbeat, it grows more sheer,
> Until in love's light, it vanishes without a trace.
> O seeker, know this eternal truth:
> The veil is but an illusion of the mind.
> In the garden of unity, where love blooms,
> No barrier between lover and Beloved you'll find."

Commentary: This poem addresses the illusory nature of separation from the divine. In Sufi thought, the perception of separation from God is seen as a veil created by the ego. The poem suggests that through love and spiritual realization, this veil of separation dissolves, revealing the inherent unity of all existence.

10. "The Flame of Longing"

> "A flame burns bright within my chest,
> Consuming all but love's pure essence.
> It flickers with each breath I take,
> Dancing to the rhythm of the Beloved's presence.
> This fire, both torment and delight,
> Purifies the heart with its sacred heat.
> In its glow, the moth of my soul
> Circles ever closer, yearning to meet."

Commentary: The metaphor of fire is often used in Sufi poetry to represent divine love and spiritual longing. This poem portrays the dual nature of this longing - it's both painful and ecstatic. The image of the moth drawn to the flame represents the soul's irresistible attraction to the divine, even at the cost of annihilation of the self.

11. "The Garden of the Heart"

"In the secret garden of my heart,
A thousand flowers of love unfold.
Each petal a universe of beauty,
Each blossom a story left untold.
The Beloved walks in this garden,
Leaving footprints of light on the ground.
In the rustle of leaves, I hear His whisper,
In the scent of roses, His presence I've found."

Commentary: The heart as a garden is a common motif in Sufi poetry. This poem presents the heart as a place of infinite beauty and potential, where the divine presence can be experienced. The various sensory experiences in the garden - sight, sound, scent - represent different ways of perceiving the divine in creation.

12. "The Music of Silence"

"In the depths of silence, a melody plays,
A song without words, a tune without sound.
It resonates in the chambers of the heart,
Where the secrets of love abound.
Listen, O seeker, with the ear of your soul,
To this music that transcends all noise.
In its rhythm, find the pulse of creation,
In its harmony, hear the Beloved's voice."

Commentary: This poem explores the Sufi concept of inner listening. The "music of silence" represents the divine reality that can be perceived when the mind becomes still. It suggests that true understanding comes not through external sounds or words, but through inner contemplation and attunement to the divine presence.

13. "The Wine of Eternity"

"From the vineyard of the soul, I pressed
A wine that intoxicates the spirit.

One sip, and time loses all meaning,
One taste, and the heart can hear it.
The song of eternal love, pure and sweet,
Flows like nectar through every vein.
In this divine intoxication, I found
A joy that needs no refrain."

Commentary: The metaphor of wine is frequently used in Sufi poetry to represent spiritual ecstasy and divine love. This poem suggests that true intoxication comes not from external substances, but from the "wine" of spiritual realization. The dissolution of time in this state points to the eternal nature of divine reality.

14. "The Thread of Love"

"A golden thread runs through creation,
Binding all beings in its gentle embrace.
From the stars above to the earth below,
It weaves a tapestry of divine grace.
Pull on this thread, and the universe moves,
For love is the force that holds all things.
In the grand design of the Cosmic Weaver,
Each heart is a knot where eternity sings."

Commentary: This poem uses the metaphor of a thread to represent the interconnectedness of all existence through divine love. It reflects the Sufi understanding that love is the fundamental force in the universe, binding all of creation together in a harmonious whole.

15. "The Mirror of Existence"

"In every atom, a universe resides,
Each particle a mirror of the whole.
Look closely at a grain of sand,
And see reflected the Beloved's soul.
The macrocosm in the microcosm lies,
As above, so it is below.
In the drop, the ocean is contained,
In your heart, the divine light does glow."

Commentary: This poem explores the Sufi concept of the unity of existence, suggesting that the entire universe is reflected in each of its parts. It draws on the Hermetic principle "as above, so below," indicating that the same divine reality can be found in the smallest particle and the vast cosmos.

16. "The Dance of Opposites"

"Light and shadow, joy and sorrow,
In love's dance, they intertwine.
Each step a perfect balance,
In this cosmic design divine.
Embrace both laughter and tears,
For in duality, unity is found.
In the Beloved's eternal dance,
All opposites are bound."

Commentary: This poem addresses the Sufi understanding of the complementary nature of opposites. It suggests that apparent dualities are actually part of a greater unity, and that embracing both sides of any polarity leads to a more complete understanding of divine reality.

17. "The Alchemy of the Heart"

"In the crucible of the awakened heart,
Base metals of ego transmute to gold.
The fire of love, intense and pure,
Reveals treasures yet untold.
This inner alchemy, oh so subtle,
Transforms the seeker, day by day.
Until in the mirror of existence,
Only the Beloved's face holds sway."

Commentary: Alchemical imagery is often used in Sufi poetry to represent spiritual transformation. This poem portrays the heart as an alchemical crucible where the "base metals" of the ego are transformed into the "gold" of spiritual realization through the "fire" of divine love.

18. "The Ocean of Mercy"

"Dive deep into the ocean of mercy,
Where waves of forgiveness endlessly roll.
In its depths, find the pearls of wisdom,
That adorn the Beloved's infinite soul.
No sin too great, no heart too small,
For this ocean knows no bound.
In its embrace, all are welcome,
In its love, all are found."

Commentary: This poem uses the metaphor of an ocean to represent divine mercy and forgiveness. It reflects the Sufi belief in the boundless nature of divine love, which is always ready to embrace the seeker, regardless of past actions or perceived unworthiness.

19. "The Breath of the Beloved"

"With every breath, the Beloved whispers,
A love song meant for you alone.
In the inhale, hear "I am near,"
In the exhale, "You're never alone.""

This sacred breath, the gift of life,
Flows through all, a divine stream.
In its rhythm, find your true self,
Awaken from this worldly dream."

Commentary: In Sufi practice, breath awareness is often used as a form of meditation. This poem portrays each breath as a communication from the divine, emphasizing the constant presence of the Beloved. It also touches on the idea that our true nature is obscured by the "dream" of worldly existence.

20. "The Candle and the Moth"

"A candle burns in the night so dark,
Its flame a beacon of pure love.
Around it, a moth circles ever closer,
Drawn by a longing from above.
In that final moment of union,
When moth and flame become one light,
The secret of love is revealed:
In surrendering all, we gain true sight."

Commentary: The metaphor of the moth and the flame is a classic in Sufi poetry, representing the soul's attraction to the divine. This poem explores the paradox of spiritual union, where the seeker's individual identity is annihilated in the overwhelming presence of the divine, leading to a higher form of existence.

21. "The Reed Flute's Lament"

"From the reedbed, a flute was cut,
Its mournful song, a cry of separation.
"Why was I torn from my source?" it asks,
Its music, a prayer for unification.
Listen closely to this plaintive tune,
For in its notes, your story is told.
The soul's journey from divine unity,
To multiplicity, and back to the fold."

Commentary: This poem is inspired by the opening lines of Rumi's Masnavi, which speaks of the reed flute's lament. The reed represents the human soul, separated from its divine source and longing to return. The poem suggests that this sense of separation and longing for reunion is the fundamental human condition.

22. "The Invisible Thread"

"An invisible thread connects
Those who are destined to meet.
Across time, space, and circumstance,
It guides their wandering feet.
This thread may stretch or tangle,
But it will never break.
For it's woven from eternal love,
A bond no force can shake."

Commentary: This poem explores the Sufi concept of spiritual connection that transcends physical limitations. It suggests that there are deep, invisible bonds between souls that are part of the divine plan. This idea extends the concept of love beyond individual relationships to a cosmic principle of interconnectedness.

23. "The Palace of Mirrors"

"In the palace of a thousand mirrors,
Each reflection shows a different face.
Yet behind each image, great and small,
Shines the light of singular grace.
Don't be fooled by these myriad forms,
Or lost in the play of light and shade.
For in this hall of infinite reflections,
One Beloved's beauty is displayed."

Commentary: This poem uses the metaphor of a palace of mirrors to represent the multiplicity of forms in the manifest world. It suggests that despite the apparent diversity of creation, all forms are ultimately reflections of a single divine reality. This reflects the Sufi understanding of wahdat al-wujud, or the unity of existence.

24. "The Cosmic Dance"

"Stars and planets in their orbits spin,
Atoms whirl in their quantum dance.

From the vast to the infinitesimal,
All move in divine, ecstatic trance.
Join this dance with every breath,
Let your heart beat to its rhythm.
For in this cosmic choreography,
Love is both the dancer and the hymn."

Commentary: This poem draws parallels between the movements of celestial bodies and subatomic particles, portraying all motion in the universe as a form of divine dance. It invites the reader to recognize this sacred movement in their own being, suggesting that aligning with this cosmic rhythm is a way of experiencing divine love.

25. "The Seed of Potential"

"Within your heart, a seed is planted,
A divine potential, waiting to grow.
Water it with tears of longing,
Let the sun of love make it glow.
From this seed, a mighty tree will rise,
Its branches reaching for the sky.
In its shade, all souls find rest,
In its fruits, the taste of the Most High."

Commentary: Using the metaphor of a seed growing into a tree, this poem speaks to the innate divine potential within each person. It suggests that through spiritual practice (watering with tears) and divine grace (the sun of love), this potential can be realized, benefiting not just the individual but all of creation.

26. "The Alchemy of Forgiveness"

"In the laboratory of the heart,
A wondrous alchemy takes place.
Where bitter poison of resentment,
Transforms to elixir of grace.
This magic of forgiveness,
Turns enemy to dearest friend.
In its crucible of compassion,
All differences transcend."

Commentary: This poem presents forgiveness as a form of spiritual alchemy, capable of transmuting negative emotions into positive ones. It reflects the Sufi emphasis on purification of the heart and the transformative power of love and compassion.

27. "The Eternal Moment"

"Between each breath, a doorway lies,
To a realm beyond time's flow.
Where past and future cease to be,
And only Now does glow.
In this eternal moment, find
The peace that never ends.
Where lover and Beloved unite,
And every heart transcends."

Commentary: This poem explores the Sufi concept of the eternal present. It suggests that true spiritual reality exists outside of linear time, in an eternal "Now." The space between breaths is presented as a gateway to this timeless realm, where the duality of lover and Beloved dissolves.

28. "The Awakening"

"From the dream of separation,
I awoke to unity's light.
The veil of illusion lifted,
Revealing a wondrous sight.
Where once I saw division,
Now only oneness remains.
In every face, the Beloved smiles,
In every heart, love reigns."

Commentary: This final poem describes the experience of spiritual awakening or enlightenment. It portrays the shift in perception from a world of separation and duality to one of underlying unity. This realization of oneness is a central goal of the Sufi path, where the seeker recognizes the divine presence in all of creation.

These poems and their commentaries offer a comprehensive exploration of Sufi themes related to divine, eternal love. They cover a wide range of concepts including unity of existence, spiritual transformation, divine mercy, the illusory nature of separation, and the omnipresence of divine love. Each poem presents a unique perspective on these themes, inspired by but not directly copying

Rumi's style and ideas. They invite us to look beyond surface appearances, to recognize our essential nature, and to embrace the transformative power of love.

With this, we conclude our collection of Rumi's poetry. In the next section, we'll offer some final reflections on Rumi's enduring legacy and the relevance of his teachings for our contemporary world.

Conclusion: Living Rumi's Legacy

The Timeless Teachings of Rumi: Lessons from a 13th Century Poet for Modern Life

Rumi, born Jalal ad-Din Muhammad Rumi in 1207, remains one of the most celebrated poets in history. His works transcend time and culture, offering profound insights into the human experience. Rumi's ecstatic, mystical, and devotional poetry invites us to remember that we are already home, already loved, and already whole. This essay explores how Rumi's teachings can guide us in modern life, emphasizing themes of love, unity, inner peace, and the divine connection that lies within us all.

The Essence of Rumi's Poetry

Rumi's poetry is characterized by its deep spirituality and profound mysticism. His words are a testament to the transformative power of love and the boundless potential of the human spirit. Rumi's verses are not merely literary creations but are imbued with the essence of divine inspiration, aiming to awaken the soul and bring it closer to the Eternal.

One of Rumi's famous quotes encapsulates his view on love and unity:

"The wound is the place where the Light enters you."

This line reflects Rumi's belief in the transformative power of suffering and the idea that through our deepest struggles, we find our greatest strength and enlightenment.

Love: The Central Theme of Rumi's Teachings

At the heart of Rumi's teachings is the concept of divine love. For Rumi, love is not just an emotion but a spiritual force that unites all of creation. His poetry often describes the soul's journey towards divine love, emphasizing that true love is an internal experience that transcends the physical world.

In his Masnavi, Rumi writes (Rumi, Masnavi):

"Love is the astrolabe of God's mysteries."

This metaphor illustrates how love guides us to the deeper truths of existence, acting as a tool to navigate the complexities of the divine. Rumi's emphasis on love as a unifying force can teach us much about our relationships in modern life. In a world often marked by division and conflict, Rumi's vision of love as a binding, healing force is a powerful reminder of our interconnectedness.

Unity and the Oneness of Being

Rumi's poetry is replete with references to the oneness of all creation. He believed that every soul is a reflection of the divine and that all beings are interconnected. This perspective is profoundly relevant today as we grapple with global challenges that require collective action and unity.

In his Divan-e Shams-e Tabrizi, Rumi writes:

"The lamps are different, but the Light is the same; it comes from Beyond."

This quote underscores the idea that despite our apparent differences, we are all part of the same divine essence. Embracing this unity can foster greater empathy and compassion in our interactions with others. Rumi's teachings on unity also extend to the natural world. He viewed nature as a mirror reflecting the divine, urging us to recognize the sacredness of all life forms. In an age of environmental crisis, Rumi's reverence for nature offers a valuable lesson in stewardship and respect for the earth.

Inner Peace and the Journey Within

Rumi's poetry often speaks of the inner journey, the quest for self-discovery and inner peace. He believed that true contentment comes from within and that external circumstances are secondary to our inner state.

In his poem "The Guest House," Rumi writes (Rumi, The Essential Rumi):

"This being human is a guest house.

Every morning a new arrival.

A joy, a depression, a meanness,

some momentary awareness comes

as an unexpected visitor."

This poem highlights the transient nature of emotions and the importance of welcoming all experiences, both positive and negative, as part of our spiritual growth. Rumi's perspective encourages us to cultivate a sense of equanimity and acceptance, helping us navigate the ups and downs of modern life with grace.

The Divine Connection Within

A central tenet of Rumi's teachings is the idea that the divine resides within us. He believed that by turning inward, we can access a profound connection with the Eternal. This inner divinity is a source of immense strength, wisdom, and love.

In his Masnavi, Rumi writes (Rumi, The Essential Rumi):

"You are not a drop in the ocean. You are the entire ocean in a drop."

This powerful metaphor emphasizes the vast potential and divine essence within each individual. Recognizing this inner divinity can inspire us to live more authentically and compassionately.

Rumi's teachings on the divine connection within are especially relevant in our fast-paced, often materialistic society. They remind us to look beyond external achievements and material possessions and to seek fulfillment in our inner spiritual journey.

The Importance of Presence and Mindfulness

Rumi's poetry encourages us to embrace the present moment and to live with mindfulness. He believed that true happiness and enlightenment are found in the here and now, rather than in the past or future.

In his poem "This Moment," Rumi writes:

"This moment is all there is."

This simple yet profound statement serves as a reminder to cherish the present moment and to be fully present in our lives. In an age of constant distraction and digital overload, Rumi's emphasis on presence and mindfulness is a valuable antidote to our scattered attention.

Embracing Imperfection and Growth

Rumi's teachings also emphasize the importance of embracing imperfection and viewing challenges as opportunities for growth. He believed that our flaws and mistakes are integral to our spiritual journey and that true beauty lies in our ability to transform and evolve.

In his poem "The Reed Flute's Song," Rumi writes (Rumi, The Essential Rumi):

"The wound is the place where the Light enters you."

This line reminds us that our struggles and vulnerabilities are the very things that open us up to greater wisdom and understanding. Embracing our imperfections with compassion and patience can lead to profound personal growth and transformation.

The Power of Surrender and Trust

Rumi's poetry often speaks of the power of surrender and trust in the divine. He believed that by letting go of our need for control and trusting in the greater plan, we can experience a sense of peace and freedom.

In his Masnavi, Rumi writes:

"When you let go of who you are, you become who you might be."

This quote encourages us to release our rigid self-concepts and to trust in the unfolding of our lives. In a world that often values control and certainty, Rumi's teachings on surrender offer a path to greater peace and acceptance.

Conclusion

Rumi's poetry and teachings are a timeless treasure, offering profound insights into love, unity, inner peace, and the divine connection within us all. His words remind us that we are already home, already loved, and already whole. In a modern world filled with distractions and challenges, Rumi's ecstatic, mystical, and devotional poetry serves as a beacon of light, guiding us back to our true essence and the boundless love that resides within.

By embracing Rumi's wisdom, we can cultivate a deeper sense of connection, compassion, and presence in our lives. His teachings inspire us to live with greater authenticity, to recognize the divine in ourselves and others, and to navigate the complexities of modern life with grace and wisdom.

In the words of Rumi (Rumi, The Essential Rumi):

"Let yourself be silently drawn by the strange pull of what you really love. It will not lead you astray."

Let us heed this call and allow Rumi's timeless wisdom to guide us on our journey towards wholeness and divine love.

Appendix: Resources for the Rumi Devotee

1. Rumi, J. (2001). The Essential Rumi. Translated by Coleman Barks. HarperOne.

2. Schimmel, A. (1992). I Am Wind, You Are Fire: The Life and Work of Rumi. Shambhala Publications.

3. Rumi, J. (2010). Rumi: The Big Red Book. Translated by Coleman

Barks. HarperOne.

4. Rumi, J. (2001). The Masnavi, Book One. Translated by Jawid Mojaddedi. Oxford University Press.

Notes and References

Index

Author Bio

Azariah Samuel A

Azariah Samuel A is a distinguished technology entrepreneur, award-winning author, and inspiring speaker. With a passion that bridges the realms of technology and literature, Azariah has carved a unique niche for himself, blending his deep understanding of modern advancements with the timeless wisdom of classical poetry and philosophy.

Azariah's journey into the world of technology began at a young age, driven by an innate curiosity and a relentless pursuit of innovation. He founded his first tech startup while still in college, a venture that quickly gained recognition for its groundbreaking solutions and user-centric design. Over the years, Azariah has led several successful technology enterprises, consistently pushing the boundaries of what is possible in the digital age. His work has earned him numerous accolades, including prestigious awards in both entrepreneurship and innovation.

Beyond his entrepreneurial ventures, Azariah is also a prolific writer, whose works resonate with a broad audience. His writing is deeply influenced by the poetic and philosophical beauty of Rumi, the 13th-century Persian poet and mystic. Azariah's fascination with Rumi's teachings began during his formative years and has since evolved into a lifelong devotion. He has spent years studying Rumi's poetry, extracting profound insights and incorporating them into his own life and work.

Azariah's debut book, a collection of essays and reflections on the intersection of technology and spirituality, received critical acclaim and won several literary awards. His ability to distill complex technological concepts into accessible and engaging prose, while simultaneously weaving in the philosophical musings of Rumi, has endeared him to readers around the world. Azariah's writing offers a unique perspective, one that emphasizes the harmony between the modern and the ancient, the logical and the mystical.

As a speaker, Azariah is known for his captivating presence and his ability to inspire audiences. He frequently speaks at international conferences, seminars, and corporate events, where he shares his insights on technology, innovation, and the relevance of Rumi's wisdom in today's fast-paced world. His talks are a blend of technical expertise and poetic inspiration, leaving audiences with a sense of wonder and a renewed appreciation for the interconnectedness of all things.

Azariah is also a dedicated mentor and advocate for young entrepreneurs. He actively participates in various mentorship programs, providing guidance and support to aspiring innovators. His commitment to fostering the next generation of leaders is evident in his hands-on approach and his willingness to share his knowledge and experiences.

In addition to his professional pursuits, Azariah is an avid traveler and a lifelong learner. He believes in the power of exploration and the importance of continuously expanding one's horizons. Whether through reading, writing, or traveling, Azariah is constantly seeking new experiences and insights.

Azariah Samuel A can be reached through his email at azariahsamuel@gmail.com. He welcomes connections and conversations with those who share his interests in technology, literature, and the timeless wisdom of Rumi. Through his work and his words, Azariah continues to inspire and challenge us to look beyond the surface, to seek deeper truths, and to embrace the beautiful complexity of life.

Back Cover Copy

"In the realm of the heart, Rumi reigns eternal. This exquisite volume opens the treasure chest of his wisdom, inviting you to experience the intoxicating beauty of divine love and the profound insights of a true mystical master.

Journey through Rumi's life, immerse yourself in his most captivating poetry, and discover how his timeless teachings can transform your own spiritual path. With expert commentary, contextual insights, and contemplative exercises, **Mystic Ruminations** is both a celebration of Rumi's genius and a practical guide to embodying his wisdom in the modern world.

Open these pages and let your soul dance to the music of the universe that Rumi so eloquently composed. This is more than a book—it's an invitation to awakening."

The Timeless Teachings of Rumi: Lessons from a 13th Century Poet for Modern Life

Rumi, born Jalal ad-Din Muhammad Rumi in 1207, remains one of the most celebrated poets in history. His works transcend time and culture, offering profound insights into the human experience. Rumi's ecstatic, mystical, and devotional poetry invites us to remember that we are already home, already loved, and already whole. This exploration delves into how Rumi's teachings can guide us in modern life, emphasizing themes of love, unity, inner peace, and the divine connection that lies within us all.

In verses spun with mystic grace, Rumi's words create a sacred space where the soul's journey towards divine love is vividly illustrated. Through his poetry, Rumi reveals that love is the ultimate force that unites all of creation, guiding us to deeper truths and profound connections (Rumi, The Essential Rumi).

"The wound is the place where the Light enters you."

This powerful quote encapsulates Rumi's belief in the transformative power of suffering and enlightenment through struggle. Rumi's teachings on unity remind us of our interconnectedness, urging us to embrace empathy and compassion. His reflections on inner peace emphasize the importance of self-discovery and mindfulness, offering a path to true contentment (Rumi, The Essential Rumi).

"You are not a drop in the ocean. You are the entire ocean in a drop."

Recognizing the divine within ourselves inspires us to live authentically and compassionately.

Mystic Ruminations is not just a book; it's a transformative journey. Let Rumi's timeless wisdom guide you to a deeper understanding of love, unity, and the divine connection within. This volume is your invitation to awakening, urging you to embrace the present moment and the boundless love that resides within us all.

Embark on this journey with Rumi and discover the profound teachings that resonate with the timeless truths of the soul.

Book Description

"Mystic Ruminations" invites you on an enchanted journey through the timeless wisdom of Rumi, the 13th-century Sufi poet whose words continue to captivate hearts across cultures and centuries. This masterfully crafted volume weaves together Rumi's most beloved poetry with insightful commentary, bringing his mystical teachings to life for the modern seeker.

Delve into the depths of divine love, explore the alchemy of spiritual transformation, and dance in the paradoxes of existence as illuminated by Rumi's radiant verse. With a comprehensive biography, literary analysis, and thematic explorations, this book offers both newcomers and devoted followers a rich, multifaceted portrait of Rumi's life and teachings.

At the heart of this work lies a carefully curated collection of Rumi's most profound poems, presented in their finest English translations. Each verse serves as a portal to the realm of the Beloved, inviting readers to experience their own "divine flirtations and enchanted conversations with the eternal."

Whether you're a poetry lover, a spiritual seeker, or simply curious about one of history's most influential mystics, "Mystic Ruminations" offers a soul-stirring journey that will inspire, challenge, and awaken you to the depths of your own being. Open these pages and let Rumi's words become a mirror, reflecting the hidden treasures within your own heart.

Keywords

Rumi poetry, Sufi wisdom, spiritual journey, mystic love, divine union, Persian literature, Islamic mysticism, spiritual transformation, contemplative practices, poetic translation

Categories

- Poetry > Middle Eastern
- Religion & Spirituality > Islam > Sufism
- Philosophy > Eastern

Target audience: Islamic readers, Sufi practitioners, poetry lovers, spiritual seekers

Glossary

1. Sufism: Islamic mysticism focusing on direct personal experience of God.

2. Ghazal: A form of Persian poetry, often expressing love and longing.

3. Masnavi: Rumi's spiritual epic poem, also known as "The Spiritual Couplets."

4. Divan: A collection of poems, particularly in Persian literature.

5. Sama: Sufi whirling dance practice, associated with Rumi and the Mevlevi order.

6. Fana: The Sufi concept of annihilation of the self in the Divine.

7. Baqa: Subsistence in God, often following the state of fana.

8. Tawhid: The Islamic concept of the oneness of God.

9. Dhikr: Remembrance of God, often through repetitive prayer or meditation.

10. Shams of Tabriz: Rumi's spiritual mentor and inspiration for much of his poetry.

11. Mathnawi: Another spelling for Masnavi, Rumi's spiritual masterpiece.

12. Mevlevi Order: Sufi order founded by Rumi's followers, known for the whirling dervishes.

13. Dervish: A Sufi aspirant, often associated with ascetic practices.

14. Ishq: Divine love or passion in Sufi terminology.

15. Tariqa: Sufi spiritual path or order.

16. Murshid: Sufi spiritual guide or teacher.

17. Murid: Sufi disciple or student.

18. Wahdat al-wujud: Unity of existence, a key concept in Ibn Arabi's philosophy.

19. Qalb: The heart, considered the seat of spiritual perception in Sufism.

20. Zikr: Another spelling for dhikr, remembrance of God.

21. Sema: Another spelling for sama, the whirling meditation practice.

22. Nafs: The self or ego in Sufi psychology.

23. Barakah: Spiritual blessing or grace.

24. Khalwat: Spiritual retreat or seclusion in Sufi practice.

25. Tariqa: Sufi spiritual path or method.

26. Fanaa: Another spelling for fana, annihilation of the self.

27. Baqaa: Another spelling for baqa, subsistence in God.

28. Wali: A friend of God or saint in Sufi tradition.

29. Kashf: Spiritual unveiling or direct perception of divine realities.

30. Hulul: Divine indwelling or incarnation, a concept in some Sufi thought.

31. Tajalli: Divine self-disclosure or manifestation in Sufi thought.

32. Qutb: The spiritual axis or pole in Sufi cosmology.

33. Maqam: Spiritual station or stage on the Sufi path.

34. Hal: Spiritual state or temporary experience in Sufism.

35. Shaikh: Spiritual master or teacher in Sufi tradition.

36. Silsila: Spiritual lineage or chain of transmission in Sufism.

37. Baraka: Blessing or spiritual influence.

38. Ihsan: Spiritual excellence or beauty in action.

39. Faqr: Spiritual poverty or detachment from worldly possessions.

40. Tawakkul: Trust in God or divine providence.

41. Tawhid: The doctrine of divine unity in Islam.

42. Shirk: The sin of idolatry or associating partners with God.

43. Muraqaba: Sufi meditation practice.

44. Tawba: Repentance or turning back to God.

45. Wajd: Ecstasy or spiritual rapture in Sufism.

46. Nafs al-ammara: The lower self or ego in Sufi psychology.

47. Nafs al-lawwama: The self-reproaching soul in Sufi psychology.

48. Nafs al-mutma'inna: The tranquil soul in Sufi psychology.

49. Ruh: The spirit or divine spark within the human being.

50. Qalb: The heart, considered the center of spiritual perception.

51. Sirr: The innermost secret or core of the human being.

52. Khafi: The hidden aspect of the soul in Sufi psychology.

53. Akhfa: The most hidden aspect of the soul in Sufi psychology.

54. Lataif: Subtle spiritual organs or centers in Sufi practice.

55. Karamat: Spiritual gifts or miracles attributed to saints.

56. Wahdat al-shuhud: Unity of witnessing in Sufi philosophy.

57. Maqam al-fana: The station of annihilation in Sufism.

58. Maqam al-baqa: The station of subsistence in God in Sufism.

59. Jam: Spiritual gathering or assembly in Sufi practice.

60. Khanqah: Sufi spiritual center or lodge.

About the Author

Azariah Samuel is a devoted scholar of Sufi poetry and Islamic mysticism, with a particular passion for the works of Rumi. Azariah Samuel has spent decades immersed in the study and practice of contemplative traditions from both East and West.

As a gifted translator and interpreter of mystical texts, Azariah Samuel brings a rare combination of academic rigor and spiritual sensitivity to this exploration of Rumi's teachings.